Prayer
A Force that Causes Change

Effective in Prayer
VOLUME FOUR

DAVID WILLIAMSON

Trafford
PUBLISHING

Note for Librarians: A cataloguing record for this book is available from Library
and Archives Canada at www.collectionscanada.ca/amicus/index-e.html

Printed in Victoria, BC, Canada.

ISBN: 978-1-4269-2774-4 (sc)
ISBN: 978-1-4269-2775-1 (dj)

Library of Congress Control Number: 2010902465

*Our mission is to efficiently provide the world's finest, most comprehensive
book publishing service, enabling every author to experience success.
To find out how to publish your book, your way, and have it available
worldwide, visit us online at www.trafford.com*

Trafford rev. 3/5/2010

 PUBLISHING™ www.trafford.com

North America & international
toll-free: 1 888 232 4444 (USA & Canada)
phone: 250 383 6864 ♦ fax: 812 355 4082

DEDICATION

To my wife, Kathy, my faithful supporter and partner, and my son, Nathan, my joy and great friend, I dedicate this book.

I wish to include a thank you to several people special to this book and ministry.

To Kathy, thank you for your hard work in getting all my newsletters out.

To the many subscribers to the *Voice of Thanksgiving, Stimme der Dankbarkeit,* and *Głos Dziękczynienia* newsletters, thank you for your support, comments, and encouragement over the years.

And a special heart felt thank you, to my translators. Thank you for your labors. You have worked long and hard, turning my English words into something very beautiful and readable, opening the door for many more readers.

TABLE OF CONTENTS

Introduction:

A VISION FOR EFFECTIVE PRAYER

And you will hear of wars and rumors of wars. See that you are not troubled; for all these things must come to pass, but the end is not yet. For nation will rise against nation, and kingdom against kingdom. And there will be famines, pestilences, and earthquakes in various places. All these are the beginning of sorrows. Then they will deliver you up to tribulation and kill you, and you will be hated by all nations for My name's sake. And then many will be offended, will betray one another, and will hate one another. Then many false prophets will rise up and deceive many. And because lawlessness will abound, the love of many will grow cold. But he who endures to the end shall be saved. And this gospel of the kingdom will be preached in all the world as a witness to all the nations, and then the end will come.

MATTHEW 24:6-14 (NKJV)

Wars, famines, pestilence, and earthquakes in various places, these were predicted by Jesus and are to be expected in the end times. We live in a time marked by an increase in these types of things. Daily we hear of wars and rumor of wars. There are famines and pestilence racing unchecked through countries. Never in recorded history have there been so many disasters such as earthquakes. And Jesus said, "…and then the end will come".

In the mist of disasters we also see special moments, times when people do things that remind us that people can be heroic, if even for only a moment. There are many stories of things people have done for others. People reaching out to help others in their moment of need, rising above their reaction for self preservation, they do something unusual and this captures our attention. Sometimes, especially with all of our high tech communications today, these heroic deeds come to the attention of people around the world.

For example, in the opening ceremony of the 2008 Beijing Olympic Games, Yao Ming, a professional basketball star and Lin Hao helped carried the Olympic torch. Yao Ming is more than seven feet tall and Lin Hao was a 9 year old student, who looked tiny beside him. Lin Hao was a student at a school destroyed in an earthquake in Yingxiu, China. His school collapsed and Lin Hao went back in to rescue two classmates. In a moment his story was flashed around the world.

There are many stories like Lin Hao, where someone has done something special or extraordinary and become a hero. Great books, poems, movies, and plays have been written about special moments and the great things people do. We hear so much that is negative that it is refreshing to hear about special moments of heroic deeds.

When God formed you, even before you were born, He put a heroic plan in your heart. By definition this means that God put in your heart a grand, noble, large, powerful, potent, and impressive in its effect, plan. It is unique and very special. And while your story may not be broadcast on TV or flashed world wide on the internet, it is intended to be heroic. One part of the plan is for you to pray and have effective prayers. Someday we all will give an account before God of our life and what we have done. Will the fruit of your prayers extract from God a Response of, "Well done", or just, "Well...?"

> *Therefore we also, since we are surrounded by so great a cloud of witnesses, let us lay aside every weight, and the sin which so easily ensnares us, and let us run with endurance the race that is set before us, looking unto Jesus, the author and finisher of our faith, who for the joy that was set before Him endured the cross, despising the shame, and has sat down at the right hand of the throne of God.*
>
> HEBREWS 12:1-2 (NKJV)

Today we need heroes. We need men and women, boys and girls doing extraordinary things. As we see the end of time approaching, there will be more and more opportunities like that of Lin Hao. There will also be more and more opportunities for effective prayer. The world we live in is scary and dangerous; the destiny of people and nations hangs in the balance and a great need is for men and women who can and will pray effective prayers.

> *Not that I have already attained, or am already perfected; but I press on, that I may lay hold of that for which Christ Jesus has also laid hold of me. Brethren, I*

do not count myself to have apprehended; but one thing I do, forgetting those things which are behind and reaching forward to those things which are ahead, I press toward the goal for the prize of the upward call of God in Christ Jesus. Therefore let us, as many as are mature, have this mind; and if in anything you think otherwise, God will reveal even this to you.

PHILIPPIANS 3:12-15 (NKJV)

Will you be a hero of the faith and respond to His call for effective prayer? Perhaps He is waiting for you to join with Him in bringing light to dark places, healing to the sick, deliverance to captives, soundness to the broken, homes to the homeless, love to the hated, and salvation to the lost. Will you pray?

Let us pray!

The articles in this book are a proclamation of what can be done with effective prayer and call for effective prayer. A life of effective prayer is one of close relationship to God and life with answers to prayers. God has given the right to draw near to Him, to take hold of His strength and be powerful in prayer. Come and explore this often forgotten treasure house of effective prayer.

This book is a series of articles that first appeared in a weekly online newsletter *Voice of Thanksgiving* over the course of several years, so there will be some repetition and redundancy of Bible verses and other info.

A CALL TO EFFECTIVE PRAYER

And he spake a parable unto them to this end, that men
ought always to pray, and not to faint;

LUKE 18:1

Jesus told His disciples that they should pray. At first glance prayer seems so simple, so why does He tell them not to faint? The answer is, there is more to prayer than first meets the eye, it can be hard work. We know we should pray, but often there are questions about, what should we pray or how should we pray? To help us sort this out, let us look at four general areas for prayer. These four areas are not in a special order, each is important, and all four should be a regular part of our prayer life.

Prayers for Needs

Our Father … give us this day our daily needs, is not drudgery for our Father, it is His delight to provide. As earthly fathers we are poor examples of our heavenly Father, but we delight to provide for our children. It is a source of satisfaction to provide. This is also true for our Heavenly Father; He is pleased to provide for our every need.

One aspect of our prayer life is to ask for and receive the meeting of our daily needs. Walking in this daily practice is important for the supply of our needs and for building and maintaining our relationship with our Father. Every day we are reminded that He is our Father and our provider. Every day we need to practice; we ask and He answers. We must always guard against the loss of this aspect of prayer.

Prayers for Family

Christianity is about relationship, with God and man. Our prayer life must include prayers for those in relationship with us. Our prayers must go beyond, "God bless me, my wife, and our kids, us four and no more." Our family is more than just our immediate family, but like the rings from the splash made by a rock thrown in a pool of water, the family we pray for, should be ever-increasing in size.

Our family, our extended families, our church families, and the family of ministries we support, these are the members of our family. Prayer for this larger family is the beginning of a ministry of prayer. Our eyes come off our needs and begin to deal with God's call of compassion, His call for caring for the needs of others. When we pray for our needs, we explore His provision. Prayer for families explores relationship and love.

Prayers by Command

God has called Christians to be involved with the world around us, it is a command. And fulfillment of His command requires prayer. Examples of fulfilling this type of command include responding to His call to pray for our leaders and the call to pray for laborers working to bring men and women to Christ. In this area, prayer is often for people we do not know or may never meet and nations we may never get to visit. This is God opening new vistas for our prayers. Prayer for family is prayer of relationship and love, prayer by command is prayer of obedience.

> *I exhort therefore, that, first of all, supplications, prayers, intercessions, and giving of thanks, be made for all men; For kings, and for all that are in authority; that we may lead a quiet and peaceable life in all godliness and honesty. For this is good and acceptable in the sight of God our Saviour; Who will have all men to be saved, and to come unto the knowledge of the truth.*
>
> I TIMOTHY 2:1-4

> *Then saith he unto his disciples, The harvest truly is plenteous, but the labourers are few; Pray ye therefore the Lord of the harvest, that he will send forth labourers into his harvest.*
>
> MATTHEW 9:37-38

Prayers of His Heart

When we come to our Father in prayer, He draws us close, even as an earthly father would hold us close. He longs for us to draw near. As we draw near, the cares of the world fall away in the strength of His power and love. This opens the way to hear His voice and He draws us so close we even hear

His heartbeat. Isaiah is an example of hearing and responding to the heart of God. When he heard the voice of the Lord (see Isaiah chapter six), his response was, send me.

The heartbeat of God is for the lost. Every prayer from His heart will include some aspect of winning the lost, drawing men and women to Him, and the efforts to reach out to others. This includes prayer for outreaches, missions, and ministries, and prayer for salvation of specific individuals. Prayers from His heart will draw us away from self. His heartbeat becomes ours and we cry out for the lost. Prayer of His heart is a sacrifice of paying whatever the price.

There you have it, four general areas of prayer. In responding to God's call for prayer we need to have all four active in our prayer life. We also need to be growing and maturing in our practice of prayer. Remember Jesus said we should pray, we need to work hard at prayer, and not faint. He is calling, what is your response? Will you say yes Lord and pray?

Let us pray!

The articles of Unit One, *A Call to Effective Prayer,* look at His call and dealing with the many needs of today. There are many areas where we need prayer, individuals, families, churches, and nations. All of these can only be successful, if they are supported by prayer.

Article 1

DREAM OF PRAYER

When I was a high school teacher I worked closely with many coaches. Over the years I learned that coaches are dreamers. Before every season they dream. They dream about what could happen with the team and they dream about the individuals on their team. They dream about their team winning a lot of games and going to the championship game and winning. The dream might be of the perfect season, or it could be of the team that comes from behind and wins in the end. The games of the season could be easy wins, showing the great superiority of the team or incredible battles fought against immense odds, and earning final victory just as the gun sounds to end the game. Hey, I told you coaches were dreamers.

They also dream about the men or women on their team. The dream here is for growth, maturity, and success in both the games and life. The good coaches are more concerned with the dreams of success for their players than dreams of the team. And often the coach who is most concerned about players wins a lot of games. So year after year, coaches dream about the team and the individuals on the team.

In prayer there is room for dreams as well. The Bible records many wonderful promises made by God. The greatest of these relates to the salvation of man. It is a great marvel that God is willing and able to deal with sin and rebellion in man. The promises given through the prophets Isaiah and others, tell us that God would send His Son, Jesus Christ, to take the punishment of mankind's wickedness and thereby provided for salvation. And God did just what He promised.

> *All we like sheep have gone astray; We have turned, every one, to his own way; And the Lord has laid on Him the iniquity of us all.*
>
> ISAIAH 53:6 (NKJV)

After this first and greatest promise, God has also made other promises to believers. Some of these promises concern prayer. He promises to listen to and then answer prayers. This promise is so powerful, so immense in its scope and potential that most people fail to believe it is possible. And fewer still pursue the promise and its fruit. Prayer is a promise that most are satisfied with having a little, when so much is available.

My dream is that people would seeking what God has for us, seeking all He has promised, seeking His fullness and best, in prayer. This seeking to see God's promises concerning prayer fulfilled can be expressed several ways. I like to use a simple phrase, "More people praying, more prayers, and more effective prayers."

For me, the dream is, first, to have more people praying. The power of the promise is null and void for people if they do not pray. The second part of the dream is to have people praying more prayers. A life with prayer is good, a life with an abundance of prayers is better. The third part of the dream is to have abundance of prayers and for them to be effective, fervent prayers that avail much. This is my dream and I hope my dream will be fulfilled in you; that you will pray, an abundance of prayers, and they will be effective, fervent prayers that avail much.

Fulfillment of this dream will be a great blessing for individuals, the Body of Christ, and for the world. We can have a great prayer life, an effective prayer life, and if we do, it will be of great value to us and to the people around us. The dream is fulfilled in people who have a desire to grow and mature in prayer. They see where they are, where they could be, and they desire to find how to get to where God wants them to be in prayer.

Pray

We need to pray. The Bible is filled with men and women of prayer. Jesus, Paul, John, David, Solomon, Moses, Joshua, and many others prayed and called for others to pray. And nowhere in the Bible is there a restriction on who may pray. There is no IQ minimum, height standard, number of years of schooling, color or length of hair, skill with languages, or even an age requirement. Everyone may, can, and should pray. Make the dream come true, pray.

> *Now it came to pass, as He was praying in a certain place, when He ceased, that one of His disciples said to Him, "Lord, teach us to pray, as John also taught his disciples." So He said to them, "When you pray, say: Our Father in heaven, Hallowed be Your name. Your kingdom come. Your will be done On earth as it is in heaven. Give us day by day our daily bread. And forgive us our sins, For we also forgive everyone who is indebted to us. And do not lead us into temptation, But deliver us from the evil one."*
>
> LUKE 11:1-4 (NKJV)

More Prayer

To pray is good, to pray a lot, is better. There is a great need for prayer. To answer the need, we need more people praying and more prayers. One of the great campaigns of Satan today is to make people too busy, tired, stressed, or whatever, to pray. We must overcome Satan's attacks on prayer.

All of the efforts of Christian men and women, all of their work and ministry, is better, more powerful and dynamic, if birthed, bathed, and borne along by prayer. Too meet the needs we face, our personal needs, family needs, church needs, and national needs, we must have prayer, much prayer. Make the dream come true, pray and pray more and more.

> *He saw that there was no man, And wondered that there was no intercessor;*
>
> ISAIAH 59:16 (NKJV)

> *And there is no one who calls on Your name, Who stirs himself up to take hold of You;*
>
> ISAIAH 64:7 (NKJV)

More Effective Prayer

There was a man who people called Father Nash. His real name was Daniel Nash and he lived in upstate New York from 1763 to 1837. Nash, who served as a pastor in the area near his home, caught an eye ailment. His eyes were inflamed and he was almost entirely blind for about six months. He could not read or write, so he spent almost all of his time in prayer. This brought a dramatic change in his life; he became a man of prayer. He worked day and night in prayer. The focus of much of his prayer was the salvation of lost men and women.

At age 48, Nash decided to give himself totally to prayer. He spent much of his time praying for Charles Finney's meetings.

Nash became the man of prayer behind Finney, praying for revival and the ministry. And from his knees came hours of prayer and wonderful answers to his prayers.

Stories of Nash are nearly legendary, but several documented stories serve our purpose here. For example, Nash carried a prayer list. On this list were names of specific people he had made the focus of prayer. Every day and often several times a day, he would pray for these people. People described his prayers as "wonderful" and "almost miraculous", but the most important point was he prayed for the people on his list until they got saved and time after time he got answers, they were saved.

His power in prayer could be overwhelming. There was a man named Dresser who went out of his way to rail against the local revival and to swear and blaspheme if he saw Christians. He took special delight in attacking young men who had just been converted in Finney's meetings. Nash heard about Dresser and put him on his prayer list and prayed. A few days later Dresser came to the local meeting, confessed his sins, and was converted.

There were other men associated with Finney who were called to prayer, for example Abel Clary. Clary was described as a good man and an elder of the church, who had been licensed to preach, but he had a heavy burden for winning men to Christ and for prayer. The burden was so strong he gave all of his time to prayer.

Nash, and often another man or two, often this was Clary, would go quietly into towns three or four weeks before Finney was scheduled to have meetings. They would rent a room and give themselves to prayer, to much prayer, to effective prayer. They would be so burdened for the meetings and for people that they would not be seen for days. For example, Finney records the following:

> When I got to town to start a revival a lady contacted me
> who ran a boarding house. She said, "Brother Finney, do
> you know a Father Nash? He and two other men have
> been at my boarding house for the last three days, but they
> haven't eaten a bite of food. I opened the door and peeped
> in at them because I could hear them groaning, and I saw
> them down on their faces. They have been this way for
> three days, lying prostrate on the floor and groaning. I
> thought something awful must have happened to them. I
> was afraid to go in and I didn't know what to do. Would
> you please come see about them?" "No it isn't necessary," I
> replied. "They just have a spirit of travail in prayer."

From *Lectures on Revival* by Charles Finney

This was Nash's norm, travail in prayer. He did not attend
many of the meetings, but would pray for the power of the Holy
Spirit to convict people of their sins and soften their hearts, so
they would be saved. If there was opposition to the meetings,
Nash prayed harder.

When he was seen in public, Nash could be bold as well.
There was a time when some young men decided to break up
Finney's meetings. Nash had been praying nearby and stepped
out of the shadows and announced to them,

> "Now mark me, young men! God will break your ranks in
> less than one week, either by converting some of you, or
> by sending some of you to hell. He will do this certainly
> as the Lord is my God!"

Finney in relating this story tells how he thought his friend
had "lost his sense". However, by the next week the leader of the
group had come, confessed his sinful attitude, been saved, and

began to tell all his friends about Christ. Before the week was out nearly the entire group had come to Christ.

Time and space in this article do not allow other stories of Nash and Clary, nor of other men and women of effective prayer, like Brainerd, Backus, Bounds, Erskine, Edwards, Guyon, Howells, Hyde, Knox, McGready, Murray, Müller, Studd, and others. Not satisfied with the conditions around them, they gave themselves to prayer, and not just prayer, but effective, fervent prayer that avails much.

There is a high call, from God, a call to Christians to step up to effective, fervent prayer that avails much. Response to this call will be the deciding factor of success or failure of churches and ministries, families and individuals. Will you step up to the call?

Without the backing of effective prayer our attempts to touch this generation, with the Gospel, will fail. We cannot go enough, preach enough, give enough, broadcast enough, minister enough, or any of the other good things we must do to reach this generation, if we do not have effective prayer backing our efforts. Without the prayers of Father Nash there would not have been the revivals of Finney. Without the effective prayers of men and women today, stepping up to the high call of Christ concerning prayer, there will not be the revivals we so desperately want and need. I ask you to make the dream come true; pray, and pray more, and pray effective prayers that avail much. Will you pray?

Let us pray!

Article 2

RESPONSIBILITY

Growing up at our house everyone had jobs, things like washing dishes, taking out the trash, or taking the laundry to the laundry room. One of my jobs was to mow the lawn. It was a good job for me and while we had a good sized lawn, it was not too hard to do. Every week I was required to check over the mower, fill it with gas, and then mow.

In God's family, the Father gives jobs to His children. This is true for every member of the family, we all get jobs. With each job comes responsibility. The question is, as a member of the Body of Christ, for what are you responsible? Some of our responsibilities are general and some personal and specific. We are given assignments by God and He expects us to complete the job. This is true for things like sharing the Gospel message and living out the Christian life before the world.

Our realm of personal responsibility includes prayer. We have been assigned the job of praying. This job is not just praying for our personal needs, it is praying for others, both those in the Body of Christ and for those in the world. We have a responsibility to pray for the Gospel message to go to our neighbors and to every group, tribe, and nation.

God has assigned each of us a specific task. The call to prayer is a call to be responsible for getting the job done. We are called to follow in the footsteps of Paul and many others in bringing the Gospel to the people of every nation. This requires many things; among these are men and women who will be responsible in prayer for answers to meet every need for the job.

To get the job done we need men and women to go to the nations. They come by prayer. We need men and women to be senders and supporters of those who go. They come by prayer. We need massive amounts of money to send and support the ministries. It comes by prayer. We need open doors of opportunity to share the Gospel. They come by prayer. We need opposition to sharing the Gospel defeated. This comes by prayer.

Will you be responsible in prayer for a new outreach or move of God? Will you be responsible in prayer for the renewal or growth of an outreach or move of God? Will you be responsible in prayer for men and women stepping into and fulfilling their call of God? Will you be responsible in prayer for the provision for men and women responding to His call? Will you be responsible in prayer for God bringing revival to a people group, nation, or region? Will you be responsible in prayer?

Let us pray!

Article 3

WORKING FOR SUCCESS

There is an old adage, "Tell everyone you meet about Jesus, use words if you must". All over the world there are Christians working. Most live a quiet life, with no fanfare or notoriety. They go about their work in God's grace and mercy. They walk by faith and demonstrate the love of the Lord. They are Christians in action, not just name. Their immediate goals vary, but their goals are part of the broad objective of winning this generation for Jesus. Some of these people work where whole groups of people hear and respond to the Gospel message. Others are winning men and women one at a time.

With all this work going on it may seem the job will soon be done. This has happened before, think of the first generation of Christians and the work of the ministry of the first years of the Christian era. Jesus went about doing good, healing all who were sick and oppressed. He was followed by the great exploits of the first disciples; some of these are recorded in the book of Acts. The faith spread rapidly throughout the region of the Middle East and beyond. It appeared the job would soon be done. However, Jesus knew there was much to do then and there is still much to do.

> *Jesus said to them, "My food is to do the will of Him who sent Me, and to finish His work. Do you not say, 'There are still four months and then comes the harvest'? Behold, I say to you, lift up your eyes and look at the fields, for they are already white for harvest! And he who reaps receives wages, and gathers fruit for eternal life, that both he who sows and he who reaps may rejoice together.*
>
> JOHN 4:34-36 (NKJV)

As we look both around the world and close to home, things look very much the same as they did then, the fields are white for harvest. This is our generation to win for Jesus. The question is, are we up to the task? We can work and even work hard, but will it be enough? If we are going to be successful, we must work the way Jesus worked. If we work like He worked, we will make a difference for the people of our generation.

One of the keys to His work was prayer. Jesus was and is the man of prayer. When He walked here on earth, He was the man of effective, fervent prayer. Effective, fervent prayer made the difference for Him and it is the instrument of change that will make a difference for us as well.

If we learn to pray, I mean learn to pray effective faith filled prayers, we will see a change in our life, family, church, neighborhood, cities, and in the nations. This will be a real change, not a cosmetic cover, but a real change. Prayer changes the times and seasons. It brings workers to the harvest fields. It brings provision to meet the needs of ministries. It opens doors that have been closed. Prayer is a force of change and if we will dedicate ourselves to prayer, we can effectively work and reach this generation with the Gospel.

Jesus is looking for men and women who will pray. His call is to those who will not be satisfied with ordinary prayer. He wants people who will learn to pray prayers that change the world. Jesus was a man of this type of prayer. There have been others, for example Elijah.

> *Confess your trespasses to one another, and pray for one another, that you may be healed. The effective, fervent prayer of a righteous man avails much. Elijah was a man with a nature like ours, and he prayed earnestly that it would not rain; and it did not rain on the land for three years and six months. And he prayed again, and the heaven gave rain, and the earth produced its fruit.*
>
> JAMES 5:16-18 (NKJV)

Please note that the effective, fervent prayer of a righteous man avails much. Jesus is calling men and women to prayer. Are you willing to learn how to pray and how to pray more effective prayers? Are you willing to take your place, praying for the spread of the Gospel; praying for people in need? Are you willing to pray for opportunities to preach and for the change of heart of men and women? In other words will you join with others in praying for the reaching of our generation with the Gospel message?

Let us pray!

THE RICHES OF CHRIST

The world around us has many beautiful things, in nature and man made. There are beautiful mountains, seacoasts, and rivers. There are beautiful buildings, monuments, and bridges and so much more. Among the beautiful places are the castles of Europe. One example of this is the castle Neuschwanstein. It is beautiful and perhaps the most breathtaking part of this wonderful castle is the throne-room. It is resplendent with the gold, ivory, and marble. However, great as this is, there is richness in Christ Jesus that exceeds any riches known to mankind.

This is a strong statement when you consider some of the rich people of the world. *Forbes* magazine every year produces a list of the richest people in the world. Some of the totals of estimated wealth are staggering. And the people of Forbes' list are not even the richest. In the book of First Kings, King Solomon is described as surpassing all the kings of the earth in riches and wisdom. Now that is rich! However, there is richness in Christ Jesus that exceeds even Solomon's.

To me, who am less than the least of all the saints, this grace was given, that I should preach among the Gentiles the unsearchable riches of Christ,

EPHESIANS 3:8 (NKJV)

The unsearchable riches of Christ, using the meaning of the Hebrew words, is abundance so great that it is beyond finding it out totally. This is far better than being some rich man's son and having his unlimited credit card. The unsearchable riches of Christ is more than just money, it is more than just wealth, and it is more than just possessions. This is abundance beyond any need I will ever have.

One time I was in Germany at a seminar, on my day off, I went to a store to buy calendars for my family and friends in the US. I found just the right calendars; complete with beautiful pictures of Germany and Bavaria. I made my selection and went to pay for them. When I gave the clerk my VISA card she would not take it, it was not good in that store. As it turned out I had an American VISA and this store only took European Union credit cards. I had money in my accounts to pay for my purchase, but I could not make the purchase (I did finally make the purchase, but only when I was willing to use Euros). The point is my credit card did not work; it was not sufficient for the need of that moment.

Just as a pocket full of Euros was able to overcome my difficulties in buying calendars, so the unsearchable riches of Christ, can overcome the problems and needs. The money in your personal accounts or even your church accounts is not sufficient for meeting every need we face. However, we have a greater resource, we have the riches of Christ and it is more than enough. VISA claims to be accepted everywhere, but the riches of Christ is really good everywhere and even where it is not accepted!

The riches of Christ is abundance for meeting the needs of the day. It is unlimited and is made available by the grace of the Lord Jesus Christ. He became poor, so we can be rich. Do not think just of money here, that kind of thinking is too limiting, think abundance for meeting the needs, all the needs, articulated in all our prayers.

> *For you know the grace of our Lord Jesus Christ, that though He was rich, yet for your sakes He became poor, that you through His poverty might become rich.*
>
> 2 CORINTHIANS 8:9 (NKJV)

To receive a credit card we must apply. We declare our ability to pay for the debits we acquire and willingness to abide by the card company's rules and pay our debts. We receive a card and as long as we abide by their rules and continue to pay for our debts, we can use the card. The riches of Christ come by His work of grace coupled with our eyes being enlightened to an understanding of the fullness of His call toward us. This is in part, an understanding of His inheritance and the exceeding greatness of His power that He gives and which backs the riches of Christ on our behalf.

> *that the God of our Lord Jesus Christ, the Father of glory, may give to you the spirit of wisdom and revelation in the knowledge of Him, the eyes of your understanding being enlightened; that you may know what is the hope of His calling, what are the riches of the glory of His inheritance in the saints, and what is the exceeding greatness of His power toward us who believe, according to the working of His mighty power which He worked in Christ when He*

raised Him from the dead and seated Him at His right hand in the heavenly places, far above all principality and power and might and dominion, and every name that is named, not only in this age but also in that which is to come.

EPHESIANS 1:17-21 (NKJV)

And my God shall supply all your need according to His riches in glory by Christ Jesus.

PHILIPPIANS 4:19 (NKJV)

The riches of Christ is the supply for all our needs. The word, all, as used in this verse from Philippians is the unlimited nature of the riches of Christ. If you have a need, the riches of Christ, has the supply of answers for that need!

If we are to fulfill our calling in prayer, if we are going to reach the nations with the Gospel message, if we are going to do all He has called us to do, we must tap into the riches of Christ. It is only through His abundance that the needs of this generation can be met. Will you pray? Will you pray in faith, knowing you can call on God to supply all your need?

Let us pray!

NEVERTHELESS

We live in a world that loves power. Power tools are not just for professionals, they are in the kitchens, garages, workshops, yards, and other places, and now people everywhere are using them. Every year tool companies come out with their latest and greatest new tools. These new tools are faster, easier, better, and more powerful.

The seeking of power has been central to the pursuits of man for centuries. Man has made great strides in the pursuit of power. It is a long way from a cooking fire to a microwave. It is a long way from a long walk home to a SUV. However, great as the power strides have been, nothing of man, compares with the power of prayer.

Prayer is a powerful force. What force can claim something as impressive as instantly healing a sick man, raising the dead or stopping rain for three years? The Bible is filled with wonderful example of God's help in times of need and problems. That is the power of prayer.

Regardless of a person's status, rich or poor, there are problems and concerns. There are just too many problems for most people to keep up. People desire and are desperate for answers. Unfortunately, most people do not know how to get answers from God. Their prayers, if they pray at all, are empty of faith and without power, and so they do not supply the answers they need. This does not need to be the case; we can have powerful prayers.

Success in prayer is not a secret, everyone who longs to know God and His power in their life, can pray. The recipe for learning to be powerful in prayer is following God's directions. There are keys to invigorating and empowering our prayers. One of the most important is found in one of my favorite scriptures.

> *But without faith it is impossible to please Him, for he who comes to God must believe that He is, and that He is a rewarder of those who diligently seek Him.*
>
> HEBREWS 11:6 (NKJV)

Anyone who has read even a few of the *Voice of Thanksgiving* newsletters knows that I refer to this verse often. It speaks to me of the importance of faith, of seeking God, and bringing our requests and needs before Him. This verse reveals a confidence we can and must have, that God wants to reward those who pray in faith. Faith is very powerful and if we are going to have powerful prayers we must come to God with faith filled prayers.

Another key for powerful prayers, often addressed in the articles of *Voice of Thanksgiving*, is thanksgiving. Our attitude in prayer makes a difference. We are commanded to come to God with a grateful heart. A good test is to check our heart attitude and see if we are thankful for what God has done. If our prayer comes from a hardened heart and unthankful heart, we are cutting off God's answers.

> *Be anxious for nothing, but in everything by prayer and supplication, with thanksgiving, let your requests be made known to God;*
>
> PHILIPPIANS 4:6 (NKJV)

> *Continue earnestly in prayer, being vigilant in it with thanksgiving;*
>
> COLOSSIANS 4:2 (NKJV)

There is still another key to powerful prayer, one not as commonly noticed. People can come to God, in prayer, to get answers for their wants and needs however, people fear that their desires will be counter to God's plans. So they often shy away from this key. So what is this key? Power in prayer comes from praying the will of God.

There is a great wealth of information, on the subject of prayer, we can learn by studying the prayer life of Jesus. It is easy to be overwhelmed by His example and we know His record; God listens to and answers His prayers. The miraculous was and is a constant companion to His prayers. While His record is amazing and exhilarating, we can learn a great deal from Him. Look at this example of His prayer in the Garden.

> *He went a little farther and fell on His face, and prayed, saying, "O My Father, if it is possible, let this cup pass from Me; nevertheless, not as I will, but as You will."*
>
> MATTHEW 26:39 (NKJV)

We know that Jesus applied faith to His prayers and He came to the Father with thanksgiving. He applied all the keys to success in prayer, and we would be remiss, if we did not look closely at the key to the power in prayer, the Holy Spirit shares with us in this verse. Jesus prayed with great power because He prayed the will of God.

> *I delight to do Your will, O my God, And Your law is within my heart.*
>
> PSALM 40:8 (NKJV)

Never had a man had more of a reason to pray for a change of God's will. God's will, would subject Jesus to the most horrible experience any man could experience. The description, from the scriptures, makes clear that in the next few hours His experience would be terrible, ghastly, appalling, and unspeakably bad. No man would desire to take on the sin of the whole world. Every fiber of His being demanded anything other than that which was the will of God for Him for this moment. **"O My Father, if it is possible, let this cup pass from Me."**

Many people pray this type of prayer. We face things that do not please us; hard and difficult times, there are even scary things. We long for a comfortable life and do not want to follow Jesus' example. It seems as though His life, ministry, and example will lead to difficult situations. However, He completed the prayer, asking for God's will over His own. He went to the cross and now He is calling us to pick up our cross and follow Him.

> *Then Jesus said to His disciples, "If anyone desires to come after Me, let him deny himself, and take up his cross, and follow Me.*
>
> MATTHEW 16:24 (NKJV)

We talk about taking up His cross, but too often we prefer what we perceive as our good. Our selfish nature rules and dominates, thus limits our effectiveness in prayer. Effectiveness in prayer comes from joining Jesus in seeking God's will. The prayer founded on "nevertheless, not as I will, but as You will" is a prayer of great power and effect.

> *Now this is the confidence that we have in Him, that if we ask anything according to His will, He hears us. And if we know that He hears us, whatever we ask, we know that we have the petitions that we have asked of Him.*
>
> I JOHN 5:14-15 (NKJV)

We need to seek knowing and obeying the will of God. Jesus walked in complete knowledge of and obedience to the will of God. So it is not surprising that God always answered His prayers. The surprise is our reluctance to knowing and obeying the will of God and thus having answers to prayer like Jesus. The opportunity is there for us. We seem to think this is a hard thing, but in reality knowing and obeying the will of God is enlightened self interest. God knows what is good for us. He has our best in mind.

Jesus has shown us the way and provided for us to have an opportunity to walk as He walked. There are several questions we must address. Will we allow the desires of our flesh, the pride of life, and sin, to keep us from seeking to know God's will? Will we settle for a life of struggles and limitations in prayer? Will we continue in frustration by lack of answers? Will we let emptiness of provision rule our life? Or will we seek God with our whole heart; seeking to know His will for every aspect of our life, ministry, and prayers.

The answers seem obvious, but it is not a simple step to take, it was a challenge even for Jesus. However, He came to the point of *"nevertheless, not as I will, but as You will"*. We can,

with the help of the Holy Spirit, know God's will, be obedient
to His will, and pray powerful prayers.

Let us pray!

Article 6

PRAYER TEARS

Do you cry? Most people cry at times, I do. I cry easily and there are many things that make me cry. One of these is when people do great things for others. It can be a real life story reported in a movie or book, but it is even stronger if it is seen personally. Great compassions or heroic deeds touch people and they can be very emotional and bring tears.

Let me give you an example of a time when I cried. Recently I heard about a lady who gave up her very lucrative job, so she could spend all her time setting up celebrations for re-turning servicemen and women coming back from Iraq and Afghanistan, through her local airport. This report just brought tears to my eyes. This act of compassion and patriotism is extra special to me, I remember coming home from the military, at a time when no one cared and it was not even considered smart to wear a military uniform on your way home. I am not upset about my experience; I am just moved when people do great things like this lady.

Emotional moments like this, help us to know a little more about God. He cries over people because He loves us so much

29

and He is pleased when we have compassion and do special things for others. This is what life should be about. Mankind is to have the heart of the Father, His love and compassion. This is how we were designed, but since the fall of man, we only see momentary acts of love and compassion. We should have more times of the love of God manifested in our life and one of the chief places for this should be the prayer closet.

The prayer closet can be a selfish place, a place just for personal gain. Some people pray to get what they want and what they want is stuff to be consumed on their lusts. Although there are negative practices by some, the prayer closet can be and should be a place of compassion and love.

We are directed to ask for our daily needs. This is a statement of faith and a type of prayer made by a responsible person. Meeting the needs of our family is part of our expression of compassion and love. However, there is a great deal of difference between the prayer of a man who longs for more so he can consume it on his lusts, and the father seeking to provide for and bless his family.

We are also directed to pray for the needs of others. This is pouring out our God given love on our neighbors. We are directed to love them just as we love ourselves. This love longs to bring salvation to our neighbor, along with all of its blessings. Salvation is where there is nothing missing and nothing broken and this is what God wants for people and what we should be seeking, for people, in prayer.

When we pray for people it pleases the Father. He tells us through the prophet Isaiah that He had been looking for an intercessor and notes His disappointment on finding none. He is still looking today.

He saw that there was no man, And wondered that there was no intercessor; Therefore His own arm brought salvation for Him; And His own righteousness, it sustained Him.

ISAIAH 59:16 (NKJV)

He wants us to pray for others, to pray His love and compassion. The prayer for our needs is important and we need the blessing of answers from the Father. The question must be, will we pray for other people. The Father, the Son, and the Holy Spirit cry tears of love and compassion, they are asking us to join them and pray.

Of all the traits of a life like that of Jesus Christ, there is none higher and more glorious than conformity to Him in the work that now engages Him without ceasing in the Father's presence—His all-powerful intercession. The more we abide in Him and grow to be like Him, the more His priestly life will work in us. Our lives will become what His is—a life that continuously prays for people.

From *With Christ in the School of Prayer* by Andrew Murray

For out of much affliction and anguish of heart I wrote to you, with many tears, not that you should be grieved, but that you might know the love which I have so abundantly for you.

2 CORINTHIANS 2:4 (NKJV)

Let us pray!

Article 7

PERFECT AND COMPLETE

Every year there comes a time when we begin to think about the next year. This point comes earlier for some people than others. For some, thoughts about next year are dictated by work requirements. Plans must be made for what will be done in the next year. For others, thoughts of the New Year may sneak up on us and suddenly we are days or even hours from the New Year.

Some people are relatively sure they know what they will be doing for the following year. Jobs, family duties, and school often fall into this category. I always knew the days of school, vacation, and day of special tests. These were planned and agreed on months, sometimes even years, before. However, there are areas of our life that we do not know about ahead of time. We have some ideas and can make some plans, but we do not know what the New Year will bring.

If we are men and women of faith, then we can expect that we will be blessed. We can have great confidence in the promises of God and His promise to us is for blessing. His promises are surer, than money in the bank. We know

He has great plans for us this year. He has been thinking about us and His thoughts toward us are for good and an expected end.

> *For I know the thoughts that I think toward you, says*
> *the Lord, thoughts of peace and not of evil, to give you a*
> *future and a hope.*
>
> JEREMIAH 29:11 (NKJV)

God's thoughts are for our betterment, for our good, for our success, and for our future. He wants us to have a great life, the life He has planned. There may be some questions for which we need the details of His plans and it is possible that we might foolishly choose to be foolish and miss out on His best. However, I believe that the readers of *Voice of Thanksgiving* long to do God's will. They know it is for their best and are noted for their obedience to Him.

> *If you are willing and obedient, You shall eat the good of*
> *the land;*
>
> ISAIAH 1:19 (NKJV)

With God's good intent and our plans for willing obedience in mind, we can wonder about the future. We can think about this coming year without fear and dread, but anticipate even through challenges that we will enjoy great blessings. One area of the blessing God pours out on us and others is through the church. This is a good time to think about prayers for our church?

One important duty for men and women, who pray, is to pray for their church. We have a responsibility to pray for the ministers, the work and ministries of the church, and for the people of the church (both those currently attending and those who will come to make this church their home this year and in the future). This is an important part of the ministry of prayer. We are to build up the Body of Christ, first by prayer and then by a wide range of actions, from living a life of faith, loving others, sharing the Gospel, to our giving.

The effective functioning of the church depends on all parts of the church working. Very important to the proper function of a church is prayer. All a successful church does will be based on and blessed through prayer. It is the effective fervent prayers of the saints that will bring power to the ministry and effective working to all the parts. It is prayer that opens the heart of people to hear and receive the Gospel. It is prayer that brings empowerment to the pastors and teachers. It is prayer that brings provision for the needs of the church, as well as for its members. It is prayer that provides for the protection of the church. It is prayer that supports the guidance and leadership of the pastor. It is prayer that changes a church from one that somehow gets by, from year-to-year, to a church that is triumphant.

The goal of our prayers must be to support God's plans and goals for the church. This support takes diligent prayer. It is work to overcome the hindrances and obstacles that the Devil throws against a church. We must labor fervently in prayer, if the church is to be successful, the prayers must not be for our will to be done, but God's will to be done. There is no place for gossip or manipulation by the members of the church, our job is to pray for the success of the church.

Our prayers, for the people, the pastor, and the church, should include prayer that they will stand perfect and complete in all the will of God. Epaphras prayed this way for the churches in Laodicea and Hierapolis. With great zeal he prayed that the Devil would not hinder these churches, that is, the people, leadership, and ministry of these churches. He prayed that they would be complete. The word translated as complete here means of full age and perfect in labor, growth, and mental and moral character. He also prayed that they would stand perfect; this means furnished with the ability and means to satisfy and execute the tasks they were assigned.

> *Epaphras, who is one of you, a bondservant of Christ, greets you, always laboring fervently for you in prayers, that you may stand perfect and complete in all the will of God. For I bear him witness that he has a great zeal for you, and those who are in Laodicea, and those in Hierapolis.*
>
> COLOSSIANS 4:12-13 (NKJV)

Most churches have a long way to go to be fully perfect and complete. However, if we will pray, effective fervent prayers, we will see great growth, maturity, and success come to our church. Let us commit ourselves to the job of prayer. Let us pray that Jesus Christ would be glorified in our church. Let us pray that we would stand perfect and complete before God. Let us pray that the church of Jesus Christ would bring Jesus Christ to this generation.

Let us pray!

THE CITY OF OUR GOD

God has blessed me with opportunities to travel and everywhere I go people ask me where I am from. And even though I know what they will say, I always tell them the same thing; I am from Longmont, Colorado. This always gets a response of, "Where is that?" Then I respond with, "It is near Boulder". People then respond by saying that they know Boulder. Although it is not the capital of the United States, or even the capital of Colorado, people everywhere have heard of Boulder. Boulder is famous.

There are many famous cities around the world. These are places that millions of people have heard of and know where it is or at least something about it. These are cities like New York, Los Angeles, Paris, Beijing, Berlin, Innsbruck, Rio de Janeiro, and others, each known for its location, an important product or industry, as a political or cultural center, or as an important crossroads. Some are famous for good things; others are famous for bad. All have had good times and bad, they are famous, but there is one city more famous and important than all the rest, it is Jerusalem.

And to his son I will give one tribe, that My servant David may always have a lamp before Me in Jerusalem, the city which I have chosen for Myself, to put My name there.

I KINGS 11:36 (NKJV)

Jerusalem is one of the oldest cities, known to people around the world. The name brings thoughts of reverence and awe or anger and hatred. This city has been the center of the greatest kingdom of all time and the battle ground for many conflicts and wars. It is noted for great events that have taken place within its walls. For King David and Solomon it was the center of their great kingdom. For the rulers of the Roman Empire it was a stumbling block to the rule of the Middle East. For Jesus it was the place of great sacrifice and ultimate triumph.

For the last two thousand years great nations have fought over it. Politicians have wrangled and battled, but have not been up to dealing with the difficulties surrounding Jerusalem. This city has had everything except peace. Wars, destruction, and oppression have been the norm. However, through all its comings and goings, God has called for prayer for the peace of this city.

And God is still calling for prayer for Jerusalem. This call has not ended or been amended. God is seeking men and women who will pray for this special place. It is important to pray for Jerusalem for many reasons, but chief among these is obedience. It is impossible to have power in prayer, if we do not obey God's call and command. There is great power in prayer, but if we will not be obedient to God, we will not see this power. Without obedience our prayers are just noise. The willing and obedient will get answers to their prayers.

If you are willing and obedient, You shall eat the good of the land;

ISAIAH 1:19 (NKJV)

If I forget you, O Jerusalem, Let my right hand forget its skill! If I do not remember you, Let my tongue cling to the roof of my mouth--If I do not exalt Jerusalem Above my chief joy.

PSALM 137:5-6 (NKJV)

We also pray for Jerusalem, to repay a great debt. We owe so much to the Jews and what God has done through them, it is only right that we should pray for Jerusalem. From the Jews we have the Old Testament and examples of great men of faith like Abraham. The city itself came through the Jewish nation with King David and Solomon. Jesus, our Lord, was born and raised as a Jew. His life of obedience and faith, as He was growing up, was impossible except in a Jewish family. We are indebted to the Jews and Jerusalem for so much, surely we should pray.

What shall I render to the Lord For all His benefits toward me?

PSALM 116:12 (NKJV)

It pleased them indeed, and they are their debtors. For if the Gentiles have been partakers of their spiritual things, their duty is also to minister to them in material things.

ROMANS 15:27 (NKJV)

It is also good to pray for Jerusalem, because it is good for us. It is enlightened self interest to pray for this city. There is a blessing, God promises prosperity and good to those who will pray for Jerusalem. When we pray, God breaks through our problems and brings us His blessings.

> *Pray for the peace of Jerusalem: "May they prosper who love you. Peace be within your walls, Prosperity within your palaces." For the sake of my brethren and companions, I will now say, "Peace be within you." Because of the house of the Lord our God I will seek your good.*
>
> PSALM 122:6-9 (NKJV)

We also pray for Jerusalem, for peace. True peace will only come to the world from Jerusalem. Just as salvation came from Jerusalem, through the death and resurrection of Jesus, so peace can and will only come from Jerusalem. Real peace, the peace of God, comes to Jerusalem and will bring peace to the world. Until this happens there will be wars and conflicts around the world.

The peace of God is real peace. Far more than just the lack of war, his peace is full and complete. The Hebrew word for peace is shalom; it speaks of well being, completeness, and welfare. It has been described as "nothing broken, nothing missing". For self, family, and nation to have nothing missing and nothing broken would be true peace. When this kind of peace comes to Jerusalem, then it can come to us. So pray for the peace of Jerusalem.

> *You will arise and have mercy on Zion; For the time to favor her, Yes, the set time, has come. For Your servants take pleasure in her stones, And show favor to her dust. So the nations shall fear the name of the Lord, And all the kings of the earth Your glory. For the Lord shall build up Zion; He shall appear in His glory. He shall regard*

the prayer of the destitute, And shall not despise their prayer.

PSALM 102:13-17 (NKJV)

I have set watchmen on your walls, O Jerusalem; They shall never hold their peace day or night. You who make mention of the Lord, do not keep silent, And give Him no rest till He establishes And till He makes Jerusalem a praise in the earth.

ISAIAH 62:6-7 (NKJV)

Let us pray!

Article 9

BREAKTHROUGH

The Bible is a wonderful collection of stories. When I was a boy many of these stories caught my attention. The Gospel accounts include stories so compelling as to grip me with the power and love of Jesus and His ministry. How could anyone help being touched by Jesus stopping under the tree and calling to Zacchaeus? How can anyone help but be thrilled when our Lord presents the little girl who had been dead, back to her parents, alive and well. It takes a callused heart not to marvel at the disciple's delivery of armfuls of bread and fish, to group after group of people, as they feed thousands of people.

One that always caught my attention was the story of the four men bringing their ill friend to see Jesus. They carried him on a mat, but when they got to the place where Jesus was speaking they could not get in. They went up on the roof and lowered the man down in front of Jesus and their faith in action got their friend healed!

> *And again He entered Capernaum after some days, and*
> *it was heard that He was in the house. Immediately many*

gathered together, so that there was no longer room to receive them, not even near the door. And He preached the word to them. Then they came to Him, bringing a paralytic who was carried by four men. And when they could not come near Him because of the crowd, they uncovered the roof where He was. So when they had broken through, they let down the bed on which the paralytic was lying. When Jesus saw their faith, He said to the paralytic, "Son, your sins are forgiven you."

MARK 2:1-5 (NKJV)

"I say to you, arise, take up your bed, and go to your house." Immediately he arose, took up the bed, and went out in the presence of them all, so that all were amazed and glorified God, saying, "We never saw anything like this!"

MARK 2:11-12 (NKJV)

There are many important keys to Christian life and for successful prayer. Perhaps today we should focus on one of the keys. A key found in this story.

This story is so visual and this made the story very interesting to me as a boy; the men broke through the roof. I never wondered what type of mat they used or if they tried to fight their way in through the crowd or how far they carried this man. My thoughts always turned to breaking through the roof. As a boy I wondered what the owner of the house had to say about this. I wondered if Jesus stopped preaching and just watched as they worked away. I wondered if the people who had pressed in to get the best seats were mad because the guys were dumping roofing materials on them.

Okay I thought about strange things sometimes when I was young, and I sometimes still do. But an important key for effective prayer is for us to focus today on one point. These were men of faith and they broke through the roof to get a breakthrough.

They had, by faith, decided to take their friend to see Jesus. These men believed that if they could get their friend to Jesus, Jesus would heal him. That was faith in action. They went to the meeting; that was faith in action. The meeting was packed out; there was no way for them to do what they wanted to do. But faith in action would not take no for an answer. And you know how they acted on their faith. There were plenty of opportunities for them to be stopped. There were many opportunities for them to give-up. But they broke through to get a breakthrough for their friend.

They broke through more than just the roof. They broke through every barrier to faith and action. In the same manor they broke through, we need to breakthrough in faith and action. Just as their friend needed the breakthrough so people today are desperate for help. In many situations there is no real hope except for a breakthrough. Just getting by is not enough, we must have something more. We must have breakthroughs.

For us to meet the needs of today we must have breakthroughs; business as usual is not enough. Trying harder is not enough. Good intentions are not enough. More meetings are not enough. The use of technology is not enough. Prayer is a force of change in this world; we pray and get answers from God, we must have breakthroughs, and they come through effective prayer.

Paul knew about breaking through. He lived a life filled with breakthroughs. Time-after-time from the moment of his conversion to the time of his death, he had breakthroughs. He also knew the source of his breakthroughs; they came from prayer by the power of Jesus Christ. For us it is the same, breakthroughs come from Jesus Christ in answer to prayers.

> *For I know that this will turn out for my deliverance*
> *through your prayer and the supply of the Spirit of Jesus*
> *Christ,*
>
> PHILIPPIANS 1:19 (NKJV)

Paul was telling the Philippians, the problems he faced would be overcome. As the Philippians joined with Jesus, who ever lives to make intercession, and prayed for Paul, Paul was confident breakthrough would come. Paul had seen it time and again, prayer followed by breakthrough. Through out Christian history this principle has been repeated; Christians have prayed and experienced breakthroughs.

However, too often people have been satisfied with the status quo and have missed breakthroughs. If we are going to be effective in prayer we must guard against anemic expectations. Remember the men of our story; they would not be deterred from their goal. They were going to get their friend to Jesus even if they had to tear the roof off the house! You can almost hear them, "My friend, you are going to see Jesus this night. We do not care what it takes, it is going to happen!" They would not be deterred. And they got a breakthrough, their friend was healed!

In our life, our family, our church, our business, and our ministry, we cannot continue with the daily norm, to seeking to just get by, we must have breakthroughs. By prayer and the supply of Jesus Christ, we can reach this generation for Christ. We can turn darkness into the light of life in Christ Jesus. We can reach out and win souls from every nation.

Breakthroughs can come for us just as it did for the men breaking through the roof. Look at the steps they followed to get to the point of having this need met; that is getting their friend healed. First, they heard the Word of the Lord. The word on the street was; Jesus heals. Second, they believed the Word and they acted on it. They believed Jesus would heal, if they could get their friend to Him. So they took him to Jesus. Third, they were men of faith and they put their faith into action. Fourth, they would not be deterred; there was no hindrance that could stop them. Fifth, God met them at the point where their need and faith met. If we follow their pattern, God will meet us with breakthroughs at our point of need.

To accomplish this we need to pray and we must not pray as we have in the past, we must demand breakthrough. John Knox reached a point where he had to have breakthrough. His cry "Give me Scotland or I die!" and he had breakthrough! How about you? Will you give yourself to prayer? Will you demand of yourself effective, fervent prayer? Will you stop being satisfied with prayer just for the status quo? Will you have breakthroughs?

Let us pray!

Unit Two

PREPARATION FOR EFFECTIVE PRAYER

I love to go camping with my good friend Mark. He is fun to be with and knowledgeable of flowers, fauna, and many other things. Beyond his skill and expertise as a camper, he is always prepared to deal with whatever comes up while camping. Let me give you an example.

One year while camping with a group of young people, we hiked into a local wilderness area. The area was beautiful, the sky was deep blue and the high mountain peaks seemed so close you could reach out and touch them. Everything seemed perfect however, being the good leader, he was, and is, when we stopped for a break Mark asked how everyone was doing. Most of the people were fine, but then there were a couple of young people who when asked, noted a mild burning sensation on their feet.

As an experienced guide, Mark knew this could be a sign of trouble, so he began checking everyone's feet. Sure enough several young people had the beginnings of blisters. Mark knew what to do and was prepared. He treated the blisters and because of his diligence and preparation, everyone was able to continue the trip without pain and suffering.

If we are going to respond to the call for effective prayer, we need to be prepared to be useful in prayer and ready for action. Effective prayer is by faith and whenever faith is involved there will be hindrances, but good preparation will deal with hindrances. Effective prayer brings answers from God and the Devil will fight against this. If we are going to be effective in prayer we must also be prepared to fight and win.

Let us pray!

The articles in Unit Two, *Preparation for Effective Prayer,* deal with many aspects of our preparation for prayer. We need preparation to deal with the needs and desires of our nature and will. We need preparation to walk in faith and love. We need preparation to withstand the attacks of the Devil. We need preparation to be strong in the Lord and in His might. We need preparation so we can pray effective prayers.

Article 10

PRAYER MASK

Several times each year, students from the high school where I worked, presented a play or musical. One year the play presented was a western and there were not enough male actors for all the male parts. One of the larger parts was that of the sheriff and this role was played by a female student. With her hair pulled back and tucked up under her cowboy hat and a big paste on mustache, she looked the part. She is a good actor and did a great job with this role.

After the play all of the members of the cast, still in costume, and stage crew come out to the lobby of the auditorium to meet with parents and visitors. This is always a fun time with students and parents. As an administrator of the school I was there to support the students, to supervise the event, and enjoy time with the students.

The girl who played the sheriff greeted her family members and several friends and then came to see me. In character as the sheriff, in her gruff voice, she said "Thank you for coming tonight. I am happy you are here, but my mustache is better than yours!" Her handlebar mustache was very impressive and I had to agree that her mustache was better than mine. We laughed about this and then about once a week throughout the rest of the year, she would come up to me in the hallway and remind me that her mustache was better. One time, as we joked back and forth, I teased her that her mustache was better, but mine was real.

We live in a time when people love the show. Putting on a show to give the impression of success has become more important than reality. If a person can look successful, then they are viewed as being successful, even if everything is falling apart. Many people go through life with a mask covering who and what they are. It is common today for people to put on a mask of wealth, strength, beauty, power, or influence, and try to make an impression.

Everyone is affected by this problem. At work or play, presenting an image drives life. Some people recognize this mess and try to stay out from under its control. However, this is very difficult because the trouble is everywhere; the pressures of the presented image are even prevalent in the Church and in Christian life. Often what we say and do is governed by how it will affect our image. This even affects our prayer life. It is easy to take a role in prayer and present an image of whom or what you want to look like, over whom or what you are.

Sometimes we recognize this in others, they talk different in prayer or they act different at the prayer meeting. However, it can be tougher to see in our own life. Sometimes the image presented is blatant, other times it is subtle and hidden, but prayers and a prayer life of style over substance, image over reality, are not the ground for effective prayer.

Let me give you an example of some of the roles people can take in prayer. For this I will use a well known story from the Bible, the story of the Prodigal Son. The roles are, the Prodigal

Son when he got his inheritance, the older brother, or the Prodigal Son when he returned to his father.

The Prodigal Son took all that was his. The division of property, the portion for the older son and for all other sons, was set by specific rules. The Older son got a double portion, but he also received responsibility for taking care of his father and the household. The Prodigal Son did not steal, but took what would be his. He took it not for the glory of his father that is to be a successful son; he took his portion to consume it on the things he lusted for.

> *And the younger of them said to his father, 'Father, give me the portion of goods that falls to me.' So he divided to them his livelihood.*
>
> LUKE 15:12 (NKJV)

The older brother wore the mask of religion; he worked hard, but also made sure that everyone knew he worked hard. He worked hard, but only as a duty. His wage was due to him for his work and his work gave him an image of being successful, but he did not have real success. His work was not for the glory of his father, which is to be a successful son. So while he had much, he failed to receive the blessing that could have been His.

> *So he answered and said to his father, 'Lo, these many years I have been serving you; I never transgressed your commandment at any time; and yet you never gave me a young goat, that I might make merry with my friends.*
>
> LUKE 15:29 (NKJV)

Too often people take on a form of one of these roles in their prayers and prayer life. Among the people who do pray, there are people who want prayer to be like a good credit card from a rich uncle, a card with unlimited usage and unlimited balance. People never admit this, being careful to adorn their prayers with good sounding words and pious expressions. However, their prayers, even their prayers for other people, are just a mask. Their true desire and fervency in prayer is reserved for getting what they want.

Please note that God desires to bless us, He is pleased to see His children prosper in all things (see 3 John 1:2), but what is our priority and heart attitude? Jesus commands us to seek first the things of God over our personal wants and needs. We need to ask ourselves: Are we like the Prodigal Son. Making our demands and seeking first our wants? Does this type of covetousness reside in us? Are our prayers tainted with seeking our good first and foremost?

The second role, the older brother type, is also very common. He is an example of a person caught up in religion, a religion of works. He is earning his way to what he wants. Did you notice what he says, "I have been serving you; I never transgressed your commandment at any time." He is all about rules and work. He also sees himself as righteous because of what he has done. This is the mask of religion; people working and trusting in their rules and position.

In prayer this is common as well. Jesus spoke of this position in relationship to prayer, in the parable of the Pharisee and the Tax Collector. The Pharisee prayed, "God I thank you that I am not like other men." This is just like what the older brother was expressing. Thank God I am not like that other son, how can you honor him. In prayer this position may be covered by good sounding prayers, but the heart is proud of self. This position is a form of hypocrisy.

Our English words hypocrite and hypocrisy are derived directly from the Greek word, hupokrites, which means "actor." This is the essence of hypocricy: putting on a religious act. Probably no sin is more common among religious people than hypocrisy. In fact some forms of religion almost demand it.

From *Rules of Engagement* by Derek Prince

There is a third position we can take. The Prodigal Son when he returned and chose to be a servant. Before he could ask for a position as a servant, he was restored by his father, as a son, but the heart attitude came without the pride of life because he was seeking to be a servant.

Suddenly, by his actions and that of his father, this son had taken on two of the most powerful roles possible in life and prayer, he was now a servant and son. Jesus walked in these two and has made provision so we can walk in them as well. Walking honestly and fully in these roles is an important key to success in prayer.

God has made us to be a son or daughter, this is not something we can earn, but is a gift from God, by His grace. There is no position that can compare to the position of son or daughter. Jesus is seated beside the Father in Heaven, and we as joint heirs with Him, can be seated with Him. Jesus' role as son is to ever live to make intercession for people. He is always asking of the Father for us. His asking and receiving brings great glory to the Father. Our role as sons and daughters is to join in His intercession and ask of the Father. This asking and receiving, brings great glory to the Father. And the successful son or daughter does all they do, not for themselves, but to the glory of the Father.

Combined with this is the role of servant. Jesus chose to be a servant and so should we. One of the interesting positions in a Jewish home was the position of a servant. There is much we can learn by studying the servant, but for this study we look at just one small part of the position of servant. If a servant so desired, he could choose to be a bondservant. The master put a ring in his ear, signifying his new position, and the servant served the master forever (see Exodus 21:5-6 and Deuteronomy 15:16-17).

This is what Jesus did, He is a Son, and by choice a servant forever. And we are invited to join with Him. A servant does not choose his work, he serves and has no glory in himself; his glory is in the success and glory of the Father. Is this what we choose to do?

> *I will arise and go to my father, and will say to him,*
> *"Father, I have sinned against heaven and before you, and*
> *I am no longer worthy to be called your son. Make me*
> *like one of your hired servants."*
>
> LUKE 15:18-19 (NKJV)

Which of these roles best describes you in prayer? Unless we are careful, our prayer life can be consumed with the covetousness of this consumer world. Unless we take vigilant care, our prayer life will be religious pretence and show. Either or both of these will render powerless our prayers. However, we can be like the returning Prodigal Son and choose to be a servant. We can let God make us sons or daughters and choose to be a bondservant as well. The true servant and son role, or servant and daughter role, well performed, yields great answers to prayer.

So how can we have more of the servant and son and less of covetousness and religious pretense? There are many things we can do, but here I will mention just three. If we work at these we can have great success in removing hypocrisy from our prayer life and prayers.

To start with, the servant son or servant daughter will desire God's will over their own will. This is so logical; God knows all and His will is for our best interest, so why would we seek our own will?

This is a big question, but note three basic answers. First, some people do not know, trust, or believe that God has their best interest in mind. Second, is rebellion, mankind has, since the time in the Garden of Eden, sought to do its own thing. The third, closely tied with the second, is pride. People love to congratulate themselves and celebrate their image of what they have done, or achieved.

Yielding to God's will is a battle best fought with the aid, direction, and empowering of the Holy Spirit. Every day, often several times a day we are tested and we must seek God's will each time over our own. Jesus was tested in the wilderness and the Devil is looking for opportune times to test you and me.

Secondly, the servant son or servant daughter will seek the truth. This is a big problem today. People claim almost anything as truth. Black is called white and truth, for many people, is whatever they want to call truth. The long standing foundations and principles for individuals, families, groups, and institutions have been broken down. And without the walls of truth protecting us, we are open to a wide range of attacks by the Devil, and he is having a field day.

Jesus is the living Word of God and the Bible is the written Word of God and they always agree and are the truth. Seeking truth frees us from deception and trickery that leads men and women astray. Truth guides us and protects us, but only if we are honestly seeking truth.

And third, the servant son or servant daughter will do all for the Glory of God. This should be our goal and our measuring rod, to be like Jesus and do all for the glory of God. And our success in this is the measuring rod of testing the success of our walk with Him. Seeking His glory is imperative in our daily walk, and if we desire success in prayer, it must be true in our prayer life. If we test all we say and do by this measure, is this done or said to the glory of God, we will walk in servant hood and son ship?

What role will we play? Are we content to seek the fulfillment of our lusts? Are we willing to hide behind a mask of religion and false piety, while living far from the standard and success of God in life and prayer? Or do we desire to come to God as sons or daughters seeking to serve God and His glory forever in life and prayer?

Let us pray!

Article 11

MATURITY IN PRAYER

One of the benefits of working in a high school is the opportunity to go to the graduation ceremony. I like the pomp and circumstance, but even more, it is great to see boys and girls who have become more mature and are now young men and women. At the ceremony you can think back to that first day of high school. They were so nervous, struggling to look cool, yet they were so immature. Now four years later they are graduating. They are still nervous and struggling to look cool, but they are much more mature.

High school students are very interesting people; they can be mature beyond their years. They do things that surprise people; they can be caring, helpful, generous, and kind. At other times, students can be very immature and at times they do things that make you shake your head and wonder if they will ever grow up. So when you see them at graduation, dressed in gowns and receiving their diplomas, you notice the vast difference in maturity from those first days of their freshman year.

Maturity in people is important, but it is a nebulous thing. People can and often do demonstrate maturity and then turn and act just the opposite. We have all had dealings with people who were mature in years, but immature in their actions. There are even TV shows dedicated to showing home movies of people acting immature. We see them doing things and then wonder what were they thinking as they nearly kill themselves.

In dealing with people, we hesitate to deal with immature people, concerned if they can be trusted or if they will do what they say they will do. We may not get what we expect from a mature person, but there is a better chance than with someone who is immature. The more important the event, need, or action, we are dealing with, the more we seek mature interaction.

Prayer is interaction with God. He loves us passionately and His love for us began long before we are born. Most people, when they first come to the Lord, are not very mature at least in spiritual things. It takes time to learn; slowly, the Holy Spirit trains us up in the ways of Christian life. If we are willing to work with the Holy Spirit, we will mature more quickly. Some people may take longer, but the lessons continue day-by-day and year-by-year. God loves us even when we are children, but He longs for us to mature. This is especially true in prayer.

Spiritual maturity is very important, but it is often neglected. If we are going to be effective in prayer, maturing spiritually is a must. In the books of Timothy and Titus in the Bible, Paul presents the qualities we should look for in a Christian leader. These traits describe a good leader and are also a description of mature Christians and mature people of prayer. If we walk increasingly faithfully in these areas, we can pray effective, fervent prayers that avail much.

Check out some of these traits from the book of Titus. How do you stack up on this list? Is this a description of your life? Are there areas where you need to work and grow? Some of the listed traits are godliness, faith, temperance, love, self-control, endurance, personal integrity, trustworthiness, seriousness, humility, rejection of sin, considerate, harmony, peaceable, subjection to authority, and dedication to doing good.

This is quite a list and if you are like me, there are some areas that need work. In some of these traits there is a lot of room to improve, grow, and mature. With some of these traits I am okay, as long as I am not challenged. For example, I always have great self-control, as long as I am getting everything I want or no one is telling me to do something I do not want to do.

Seriously, we all need to grow and mature at least in some areas. We can make changes, learn, and be more mature. There are steps that will yield consistent good results, if applied, well... consistently. Guided and directed by the Holy Spirit, obediently following His command, we can mature in any of theses areas.

The first step is to desire to be mature. It is easy to just take life as it comes and do nothing to make changes. However, if we desire to mature and we are willing to work with the Holy Spirit, He will bring change to our life.

The second step is to ask for God's guidance, His training, and His empowerment for maturing. God desires for us to mature and is well able to help us. He understands the process and He knows the difficulties of living in this world. So He has prepared for us, all we need to mature. If we ask, He will help us.

The third step is study the Word of God. In every area where we want to make changes this is a crucial step. We must do things God's way. We can know His will and direction for so much of life's questions, if we read and study His Word, which is the final word on every subject.

The fourth step is to memorize key verses from the Bible. It would be good to focus on verses on maturing. This step is very important because we must get God's Word into our heart. It is good to read and study, but effective change comes from what is placed in our heart. If we continue to only place the world and its ways in our heart, we will not mature. If on the other hand, we place, in ever increasing amounts, God's Word in our heart by memorizing specific verses, on this or any subject, we will mature. It is important to place God's Word in our heart in abundance.

The fifth step is to declare, out loud, what God says about us and these traits. In the book of Romans we read of the process for getting things done in the spiritual world. We can follow this guidance and mature, or we can continue to do things other ways and fail to mature. It is a choice we are given. What is this process? Believe in our heart and then confess with our mouth. This is God's way and the only way for real growth in spiritual matters. This is how we got saved and it is how we mature.

> *that if you confess with your mouth the Lord Jesus and*
> *believe in your heart that God has raised Him from the*
> *dead, you will be saved.*
>
> ROMANS 10:9 (NKJV)

The sixth step is practice, practice, practice, practice, and then practice some more. We must, by the guidance of the Holy Spirit, practice doing the correct things, the correct way, over and over until they are ingrained habits of our life. Even then we must practice checking to be sure we have not gotten lazy or careless in our practices. The things of the spirit must become second nature to us, which is good to have, because this is our new nature, now that we are Born Again.

And finally, we need to follow the line from the old children's verse, if we fall, we are to, "pick our self up and start all over again". If we stumble and act immature, we can go to the Father and repent of our ways, receive His forgiveness, and begin again our lessons on maturity. We need not wallow in the mire of failure until the pigs come home for their slop, but we can come to our senses now, repent and amend our ways.

Well, there you have it, a road to maturity. I know there is much here you have heard before, but mature people do not mind being reminded of how to walk and the way to get to their planned destination. The world of today is longing for the sons and daughters of God to rise up and be mature. This is especially true in prayer. If we will walk mature in spiritual matters, we will be great in prayer and meet the needs of this generation with answers from God.

Let us pray!

Article 12

A PLATFORM FOR EFFECTIVE PRAYER

As children we spent many afternoons buying and selling property in and around Atlantic City, New Jersey. Of course the buying and selling was over the famous board game *Monopoly*. *Monopoly* is one of the best known board games of all time and includes glorious moments when someone would land on one of my properties and despair when I would land on theirs.

The game features spaces marked as properties, streets, utilities, and railroads. The game also has special spaces, one of these is a corner space labeled, "In Jail". A player landing there must serve his time before he can leave jail. The game also has spaces where you must pick a card and do what the card says. The most valuable card is the "Get Out of Jail Free" card. If you have this card and land in jail, you do not have to wait to get out. Millions of people have sat down with the man with monocle in morning dress and tried to own all the property on the board and live the good life.

65

Owning all the property in the game *Monopoly* is great; however the Christian life is much more rewarding, it is amazing. Stop for a moment and think about this great wonder. God has provided for us and by faith in Jesus, we are joint heirs with Him. God clothes us with a robe of righteousness. This is the greatest gift of all times, nothing can compare to the life we have in Him. We should and can walk like giants in the land, having life in Him and all His promises provide. This is the real good life!

> *But as many as received Him, to them He gave the right to become children of God, to those who believe in His name: who were born, not of blood, nor of the will of the flesh, nor of the will of man, but of God.*
>
> JOHN 1:12-13 (NKJV)

> *For you are all sons of God through faith in Christ Jesus. For as many of you as were baptized into Christ have put on Christ. There is neither Jew nor Greek, there is neither slave nor free, there is neither male nor female; for you are all one in Christ Jesus. And if you are Christ's, then you are Abraham's seed, and heirs according to the promise.*
>
> GALATIANS 3:26-29 (NKJV)

A lot of people do not know this gift of God. They are mired in death and destruction. They are caught up in the destructive cycle that is epitomized by the dealings of the thief; who comes to steal, kill, and destroy. This is their lot in life and try as they may with money, power, or position there is no peace for the raging war of devastation. Without hearing and receiving, by faith, the Gospel, they have no hope.

The thief does not come except to steal, and to kill, and to destroy. I have come that they may have life, and that they may have it more abundantly.

JOHN 10:10 (NKJV)

Unfortunately, many Christians fail to live the abundant life Jesus provided. They live life just like those who have no hope. One of the chief reasons for this failure is their view of the Gospel. They try to use God's gift of salvation, as a, "Get Out of Jail Free" card. Day-after-day they live like the Devil and then try to use the Gospel to get them out of their mess. They try to make the verse, I John 1:9 say, "If we do anything God does not like, He will say it is okay, ignore our sin, and fix the problems we create". However, that is not what it says. This is not the Gospel and it is not the good life God has prepared for us.

If we confess our sins, He is faithful and just to forgive us our sins and to cleanse us from all unrighteousness.

I JOHN 1:9 (NKJV)

This "Get Out of Jail Free" card mentality is not always manifested as riotous living. Sometimes this is exhibited in subtle ways. We would never rob a bank, but there are, so called, little sins that we allow to continue in our life. This is especially true in character issues. We claim that this is the way I am, there is nothing I can do about this, or this is my nature. We see the great and mighty sins of evil people as horrible, however, there are little sins we allow to remain in our life. We pick and choose what we want to obey and try to use the "Get Out of Jail Free" card to allow us to continue with our pet sins. And make excuses to justify ourselves.

This is not the Gospel of Christ and it hinders both our life and prayers. David knew this problem; David always lived his life big. When he followed God, it was with all of his heart, when he sinned he did it big. Read about David, his sin, and his attempted cover up in 2 Samuel, Chapter 12.

David stayed home from war one summer and saw the beautiful Bathsheba. He wanted her, took her, and she became pregnant. David attempted a cover-up, and ended up having Bathsheba's husband killed in battle. David then took Bathsheba as his wife.

David thought he could just live with his sin, but God knew and revealed David's sin to one and all. God sent the prophet Nathan to tell David about a rich man who stole another mans only lamb. David was angry with the rich man of the story. Then Nathan revealed that God knows and was going to hold David accountable for his sin.

> *Then Nathan said to David, "You are the man! Thus says the Lord God of Israel: 'I anointed you king over Israel, and I delivered you from the hand of Saul. I gave you your master's house and your master's wives into your keeping, and gave you the house of Israel and Judah. And if that had been too little, I also would have given you much more! Why have you despised the commandment of the Lord, to do evil in His sight? You have killed Uriah the Hittite with the sword; you have taken his wife to be your wife, and have killed him with the sword of the people of Ammon.*

2 SAMUEL 12:1-9 (NKJV)

On a much smaller, but just as evil, scale, we do the same things. We hold on to our pet sins and try to cover it up. We quote 1 John 1:9, but we do not plan to, nor do we work to make a change in our life. It is like David living in sin and his cover up. However, God will always send His "Nathan". The question is what will we do? If we repent, turn from our sin, and we are cleansed. If we try to use the "Get Out of Jail Free" card and continue in sin, we miss His blessing.

This has great bearing on our success in every aspect of the Christian life, especially prayer. David bluntly explained and made it very clear that God will not hear our prayers if we try to use the "Get Out of Jail Free" card. He said,

If I regard iniquity in my heart, The Lord will not hear

PSALM 66:18 (NKJV)

God hearing our prayer is a key to success in prayer. If we want answers to prayer, we must walk in the light of and the requirements of the Gospel message. The Gospel is not a license for sinning, but a call to walk free from sin.

This is the message which we have heard from Him and declare to you, that God is light and in Him is no darkness at all. If we say that we have fellowship with Him, and walk in darkness, we lie and do not practice the truth. But if we walk in the light as He is in the light, we have fellowship with one another, and the blood of Jesus Christ His Son cleanses us from all sin. If we say that we have no sin, we deceive ourselves, and the truth is not in us. If we confess our sins, He is faithful and just to forgive us our sins and to cleanse us from all unrighteousness. If we say that we have not sinned, we make Him a liar, and His word is not in us. My little children, these things I write to you, so that you may not sin. And if anyone sins, we have an Advocate with the Father, Jesus Christ the righteous. And He Himself is

*the propitiation for our sins, and not for ours only but
also for the whole world.*

I JOHN 1:5-2:2 (NKJV)

Every day we must pick up our cross and follow Jesus. Part
of this daily walk is repentance, confessing our sin and turning
away from sin. The great news is that God has made provision
to help us; we can depart from evil and walk in His abundant
life. When we are free from our sins and past, we can walk as
Jesus walked and boldly pray as Jesus prayed.

*The highway of the upright is to depart from evil; He who
keeps his way preserves his soul.*

PROVERBS 16:17 (NKJV)

Each day we can walk boldly through the day. With the
weight of sin off our shoulders, we can depart from evil. Jesus
expects us to confess our sin and receive forgiveness, and from
this grace and freedom, He expects us to pick up our cross and
follow Him.

Part of our daily cross carrying is walking free from sin.
We fight the good fight of faith. We resist the Devil. We lay
aside every weight and hindrance. We run the race set before
us. We present our bodies as a holy and an acceptable sacrifice
to God.

*Fight the good fight of faith, lay hold on eternal life, to
which you were also called and have confessed the good
confession in the presence of many witnesses.*

I TIMOTHY 6:12 (NKJV)

*Therefore we also, since we are surrounded by so great
a cloud of witnesses, let us lay aside every weight, and*

the sin which so easily ensnares us, and let us run with endurance the race that is set before us,

HEBREWS 12:1 (NKJV)

For whatever is born of God overcomes the world. And this is the victory that has overcome the world--our faith.

1 JOHN 5:4 (NKJV)

I beseech you therefore, brethren, by the mercies of God, that you present your bodies a living sacrifice, holy, acceptable to God, which is your reasonable service.

ROMANS 12:1 (NKJV)

The question is will we walk free from sin? There is a temptation to live with our pet sins; to go along with life as the world lives. Every day the "Get Out of Jail Free" card will be there waiting for us, calling out for us to sin and then use the card. It is a true temptation, but it is one we do not have to give into.

As a new creation in Christ, we can live in newness of life. Today, make a wise decision, pick up your cross and do not follow after that old sin. This is where we long to be and where we need to be; this is a platform for effective prayer.

Now this is the confidence that we have in Him, that if we ask anything according to His will, He hears us. And if we know that He hears us, whatever we ask, we know that we have the petitions that we have asked of Him.

1 JOHN 5:14-15 (NKJV)

We know that whoever is born of God does not sin; but he who has been born of God keeps himself, and the wicked one does not touch him. We know that we are of God, and the whole world lies under the sway of the wicked one. And we know that the Son of God has come and has given us an understanding, that we may know Him who is true; and we are in Him who is true, in His Son Jesus Christ. This is the true God and eternal life. Little children, keep yourselves from idols. Amen.

1 JOHN 5:18-21 (NKJV)

Let us pray!

Article 13

CLEAN POT

When I was a boy, my dad and I would do the dishes on Saturday nights. We helped with the dishes on other nights, but on Saturday nights we did it all. Most Saturdays this meant cleaning and polishing all of the cooking pots and pans. Mom had a set of copper bottomed pots and pans, and the copper would get tarnished with time and use. Some Saturday nights we would wash all the dishes and then dad would make some home made polish and we would begin to work on each pot and pan. When we were finished, with all resting in the drying rack, the copper bottoms would shine and look like new. This was always a source of pride for me that my dad and I could make those pots and pans look bright and new.

The Gospel is good news. Like my Dad and I did with pots and pans, the Father and His Son can make even the foulest of us look bright and new. By the blood of Jesus we can be washed clean of all our sins, we are cleansed from all unrighteousness. The Father and Son polish is perfect and complete for dealing with even the worst sinner. All who respond to the

Gospel message, all who receive Jesus as Lord are made clean and new.

> *"Come now, and let us reason together," Says the Lord, "Though your sins are like scarlet, They shall be as white as snow; Though they are red like crimson, They shall be as wool.*
>
> ISAIAH 1:18 (NKJV)

> *But if we walk in the light as He is in the light, we have fellowship with one another, and the blood of Jesus Christ His Son cleanses us from all sin.*
>
> 1 JOHN 1:7 (NKJV)

> *and from Jesus Christ, the faithful witness, the firstborn from the dead, and the ruler over the kings of the earth. To Him who loved us and washed us from our sins in His own blood,*
>
> REVELATION 1:5 (NKJV)

There is great power in prayer. Answers to prayer can change desperate needs into great blessings and provision. This power is promised by God, is appropriated by faith, and applied by prayer. This is a very powerful combination, promise, faith, and prayer.

Unfortunately there are hindrances to seeing this combination work. The Word and promises of God do not change. They are always available and always effectual. The variable, in receiving answers to our prayers, is the man or woman of prayer. Unfortunately, people do not always follow the prescription God has given for effective prayer. There are many stumbling blocks that can hinder prayer: lack of faith, unforgiveness, unbelief, doubt, and fear.

Like the pots and pans my Dad and I washed and polished, men and women of prayer can become tarnished and loose their effectiveness in prayer. One of the most common causes of this tarnishing to prayer is sin. God has called for holy living for all Christians and this is even more important for men and women longing to be effective in prayer. We cannot receive the answers we seek, if we are not clean before God.

In much the same way that Dad and I dealt with the tarnish on the pots and pans, God has a polish for cleaning those who will come to Him. It is available and effective for everyone who asks for help to be holy. Dad's polish was made of items available to everyone and his formula was very effective. God's polish is available for everyone and is very effective. Our standard was each pot and pan shining like it was new. God's standard is that we would be as white as snow, holy before Him.

With pots and pans the cleaning was easy; we would rub the copper bottoms with Dad's solution and they would shine, all clean and like new. With the Gospel message we can do something similar. There are several parts to the spiritual rubbing compound that is used to take away our tarnish and make us clean and like new.

The first ingredient in our spiritual rubbing compound is healthy doses of the Word of God. The Bible is the best guide to successful living. It has the wisdom of God and it reveals areas where we have missed the mark. And it has the remedy for all our failings. The Word of God is very powerful. It is the power source for overcoming all that hinders walking in the abundant life of the Gospel. It is the power for making changes to our life and overcoming the effects of the world, evil, and sin.

How can a young man cleanse his way? By taking heed according to Your word.

PSALM 119:9 (NKJV)

that He might sanctify and cleanse her with the washing of water by the word, that He might present her to Himself a glorious church, not having spot or wrinkle or any such thing, but that she should be holy and without blemish.

EPHESIANS 5:26-27 (NKJV)

The second ingredient is the Holy Spirit. He is very important for removing tarnish. He gives guidance and direction and so much more. He imparts grace, faith, assurance, truth, judgment, glory, and power. He works from the inside out to make us like Jesus.

And when He has come, He will convict the world of sin, and of righteousness, and of judgment: of sin, because they do not believe in Me; of righteousness, because I go to My Father and you see Me no more; of judgment, because the ruler of this world is judged.

JOHN 16:8-11 (NKJV)

Another ingredient to this spiritual rubbing compound, designed to make us clean, holy, and effective in prayer, is prayer. This seems like circular thinking or double talk, but it really is true. Prayer helps us walk clean and holy before God. So prayer helps us be effective in prayer.

One important part of prayer is relationship. Time in prayer can and should be time of building a relationship with God. Time spent with God changes a person. He is a holy God and His nature rubs off on us. The areas of our life that are not holy, are exposed in the light of His holy nature, and changed. We are changed when we are in His presence.

> *If you abide in Me, and My words abide in you, you will ask what you desire, and it shall be done for you. By this My Father is glorified, that you bear much fruit; so you will be My disciples.*
>
> JOHN 15:7-8 (NKJV)

If we are going to be effective in prayer we must walk in the cleansing of the Word, work of the Holy Spirit, and relationship building of prayer. We must make sure that we are living a life pleasing to the Father and that makes us a useful tool in ministry. We have a choice, we can be a vessel fit for the master's use, for noble purposes, or we can walk in the ways of the world. Our prayer life will bear the marks of this choice; an honorable vessel can pray effective, fervent prayers that avail much.

> *Come and hear, all you who fear God, And I will declare what He has done for my soul. I cried to Him with my mouth, And He was extolled with my tongue. If I regard iniquity in my heart, The Lord will not hear. But certainly God has heard me; He has attended to the voice of my prayer. Blessed be God, Who has not turned away my prayer, Nor His mercy from me!*
>
> PSALM 66:16-20 (NKJV)

Let us pray!

Article 14

OKAY, GUARD, AND DESIRE

When I get to visit my friends Mathias and Ursula in Germany, I also visit the ice cream stand near their house. At this stand you can get about a dozen different flavors and the biggest difficulty is deciding which flavor to buy (the pistachio, hazelnut, and lemon are wonderful!). I like ice cream and it is easy for me to make excuses for going to get ice cream, any time of the day or night. I can be creative and so it is easy for me to come up with justifications for saying it is okay to eat ice cream, but too much of this is not good.

It is important for us to review our life and practices. There are things we should be doing and things we can do better. As we see areas that need change we can, guided by the Holy Spirit, make the changes we need. This process helps us mature as a Christian, deepen our relationship with God, and fostering greater effectiveness in prayer.

There are many areas we can look at in studies on effective prayer and a successful prayer life, but for this study we will keep things very simple. We will look at three common words. These are words we use every day, but these words make for a good study. They can help us make improvements in our life and prayers.

Three Words – Okay, Guard, and Desire

The first word is okay, this is a very simple word used often by some people, it means to approve or authorize. Please note that the word okay works two ways, it can be used to approve or authorize someone to do something or to not do something. The second word in this study is guard. Guard means the act of protecting or defending. We protect and defend those things that are important to us. The third word is desire. Desire means to wish or long for something. We desire to have effective prayers.

Desire

Let us begin with desire. This is a good place to begin because it is so important. What we desire and the strength of our desire, will greatly affect our life and how we live. For example, part of an effective prayer life is drawing ever closer to God. The desire to strengthen our relationship with God is a good desire.

Part of a close relationship with God is a desire to serve. It is advantageous in many ways to be a servant. There is a great blessing in drawing near to God and serving Him. There is also great blessing in serving people.

God helps us to have a close relationship with Him, so we can know more about Him and what is important to Him. One of the things dearest to His heart is a love for people. He loves people so much He gave His son to die for them. The man or woman of effective prayer will draw close to God, hear, see, and feel His love, and in turn, will pray for people to respond to God's love. Desiring to be near God helps us, we are changed and our prayers are empowered. A good desire causes us to be blessed, so we can be a blessing.

Desire can be a strong influence on our life and prayers, unfortunately, our desire can be beaten down. Jesus taught about the sower sowing seeds and the affect of thorns. He explained that the cares of this world, the deceitfulness of riches, and desires for other things, can choke the word and make it unfruitful.

> *Now these are the ones sown among thorns; they are the ones who hear the word, and the cares of this world, the deceitfulness of riches, and the desires for other things entering in choke the word, and it becomes unfruitful.*
>
> MARK 4:18-19 (NKJV)

This same pressure, the deceitfulness of riches and the desires for other things, can affect our desire. The cares of the world, day after day, pound on our godly desires. If we are not careful they work to suppress or demolish our godly desires. The deceitfulness of riches can hinder and spoil us, changing our desires to a desire for worldly things.

The words, deceitfulness of riches, used in Jesus' teaching (Mark 4:19), means a delusion about riches. Thinking that wealth, money, possession, abundance, riches, or valuable bestowments, can supply our needs, is a delusion. Most people, consciously or subconsciously, want riches so they do not have to trust God. A desire for this delusion brings impediment to or the destruction of, our being blessed and hinders our God given desires.

If we let our desires turn to worldly desires then our prayers will be hindered. We will be caught up in the pursuit of riches, power, position, and fame. Too often people have ruined what could have been a good and effective prayer life by the influence of the world.

By contrast we can cultivate a strong desire to seek God. God has made provision for us so we do not have to seek worldly desires. We can walk with Him in purity and holiness, and have desires that seek to obtain God's plans for our life. With Godly desires we can and will work with Him to develop a holy life pleasing to Him. This opens the door to effective prayers.

Guard

If we are going to pursue Godly desires, especially desires concerning effective prayer, we must be on guard. There are hindrances working to derail our life and keep us from God and His plans. There are three main areas that we must guard; these are the main parts of a person, the body, soul, and spirit.

Guarding the body is important for success in prayer. This is an area where Eastern thinking often creeps into our thinking. Eastern philosophies teach that the body is evil and should be suppressed. However, this is not the teaching of the Bible. God made man with a body and then called this good. Unfortunately, as a consequence of the fall of man, our bodies are under the curse. We long for the day when we will receive our new bodies and be like Jesus, but until then, these bodies we have must serve us and the work we do.

Paul explains concerning our bodies what we should desire. Our bodies can be vessels for honor and useful for the master and prepared for every good work or they can be the opposite. Guarding our body is cleansing ourselves, so we can have a body of honor, useful for good work.

> *Nevertheless the solid foundation of God stands, having*
> *this seal: "The Lord knows those who are His," and,*

"Let everyone who names the name of Christ depart from iniquity." But in a great house there are not only vessels of gold and silver, but also of wood and clay, some for honor and some for dishonor. Therefore if anyone cleanses himself from the latter, he will be a vessel for honor, sanctified and useful for the Master, prepared for every good work. Flee also youthful lusts; but pursue righteousness, faith, love, peace with those who call on the Lord out of a pure heart. But avoid foolish and ignorant disputes, knowing that they generate strife. And a servant of the Lord must not quarrel but be gentle to all, able to teach, patient, in humility correcting those who are in opposition, if God perhaps will grant them repentance, so that they may know the truth, and that they may come to their senses and escape the snare of the devil, having been taken captive by him to do his will.

2 TIMOTHY 2:19-26 (NKJV)

To be useful our body must help us to live a Christian life and to do the work of God's plan for our life. When we apply this to prayer it means it must support us as we go through our daily prayers. For example if we pray for open doors of opportunity, to walk in God's answer, we must be in the right place, at the right time, and with the resources to walk through the God given open door. If our body cannot do this we are hindered from success.

We also must guard our soul which is our mind, will, and emotions. Guarding our soul is important because it affects so much in our life. Proper guarding is separation from the affect of the thorns and snares of the world that work to defeat our Godly desires.

If our mind is not renewed by the word of God we cannot have success. If our will rules over the will of God, then we cannot triumph. If our emotions rule us, casting us about from moment to moment, then we cannot prosper.

Thorns and snares are in the way of the perverse; He who guards his soul will be far from them.

PROVERBS 22:5 (NKJV)

Beloved, I pray that you may prosper in all things and be in health, just as your soul prospers.

3 JOHN 1:2 (NKJV)

Finally, we must guard our spirit. Our spirit is born again, if we have made Jesus, Lord of our life. This means we have become a new person with a new spirit. This spirit must be guarded. Spirits flourish on close relationship with God and guarding our spirit is protecting this relationship.

When we have that feeling that God is far from us, it has come from failing to guard our relationship. God has invited us to come boldly to Him; He has not limited, but encourages a close relationship. And we must guard against anything that would try to separate us from God.

Paul in Romans chapter eight gives us a long list of things that cannot separate us from the love of God. So we are safe from the threat of all of these, but the real problem is that we can choose to be separated. If we fail to be conquerors by guarding our spirit then we separate our self. Most people do not realize they have a choice and so the fall into a separation from the love of God, they no not need to have.

Yet in all these things we are more than conquerors through Him who loved us. For I am persuaded that neither death nor life, nor angels nor principalities nor powers, nor things present nor things to come, nor height nor depth, nor any other created thing, shall be able to separate us from the love of God which is in Christ Jesus our Lord.

ROMANS 8:37-39 (NKJV)

Okay

The third word in our little study is the word okay. One of the keys to successful guarding is how we deal with the giving of permission. The guard on duty at a gate of a factory does not guard well if he gives permission to enter to those who should not be given access. This guard also fails if he does not give entrance to those who should be given access. As we study desire and guarding, we must look at, to whom, what, and when we give permission, saying okay.

I shared a little about my love of ice cream at the beginning of this study. If I always okay the eating of ice cream, then I am not guarding my body. Giving my okay too often, in this case, would destroy my body's ability to support the work of prayer that God has called me to do. By contrast, I should say okay to a good diet and rest for my body, so I can fulfill the desires God has given me.

I also must guard my soul; it is receptive to the inputs it receives. If we allow it to do its own thing, the soul will run amuck, if we feed it the cares of the world or the disillusionment of riches, then it will hinder or destroy fulfillment of our desires. So I must guard the input to my soul. I cannot say okay to just anything that comes to my mind, emotions, or will.

But know this, that in the last days perilous times will come: For men will be lovers of themselves, lovers of money, boasters, proud, blasphemers, disobedient to

parents, unthankful, unholy, unloving, unforgiving,
slanderers, without self-control, brutal, despisers of
good, traitors, headstrong, haughty, lovers of pleasure
rather than lovers of God, having a form of godliness but
denying its power. And from such people turn away!

2 TIMOTHY 3:1-5 (NKJV)

I must be careful giving of my okay, so I can guard my body, soul, and spirit. Careful giving of okay, careful guarding, supports fulfilling of my God given desires. If I watch the giving of my okay, if I guard carefully spirit, soul, and body, then I can see my desires fulfilled. I can be a champion of prayer and effective in prayer.

Let us pray!

Article 15

FOR THE JOY
SET BEFORE HIM

I t was so frustrating. We were a good football team, but we were stopping ourselves from success. On every play we would make a mistake; a penalty, a dropped pass, a fumble, something to keep us from being successful. Throughout the first half of the game we continued to make mistakes and the frustration mounted.

At halftime we talked to the team about each man doing his job and not making mistakes and everything began to come together in the second half. We began to have plays where everyone did his job and we had success. Then we began to have several good plays in a row. Everything was coming together; we knew we were going to win.

We began a drive and each play you could see the team growing in confidence and assurance that each man would do his job. We had a play where our running back ran the ball for about 20 yards and he almost went for a long touchdown, but he was tripped up by the last defender. Just as he hit the ground all the lights in the stadium went out. It was just as if the crash of him hitting the ground had knocked out the lights.

Once we realized what had happened, that there was a power outage causing the lights to go out, despair came crashing down on us with even greater darkness than the stadium lights being out. We had finally gotten everything together and were doing what was needed to win the game and now this. Even if they could get the lights back on, we were concerned; would we still be able to execute our plays or would we revert back to our mistakes? With every moment the lights were out, despair got darker.

It took a long time to get the lights back on; we even went back into the locker room and talked to the team for a while. We told them to stay focused and keep their mind on the game; the lights would be back on soon. Finally the lights did come on and we warmed up again and restarted the game. And it turned out very exciting because we continued just where we had left off. Everyone on the team doing their job and we won the game easily.

That night we had a time of despair, but think about Jesus' disciples and their time of despair. Everything was coming together for the ministry. Things had progressed so slowly, however, now progress was at hand. A short time before, the small number of people following Jesus had become masses. Now there never was a quiet moment and the crowds were becoming more and more devoted to Jesus. Why there was a time a few weeks ago when the masses wanted to try and make Jesus king by force. It was all Jesus could do to disperse the crowd.

And then a few days ago the crowds had lined the road and thrown palm branches on the road before Him as He rode into Jerusalem. They shouted, "Hosanna! Blessed is He who comes in the name of the Lord, the King of Israel!" Surely, this was the time. It was the time they had dreamed about and worked for, everything was coming together, surely now Jesus would be made king.

Then with the fearsome thud of finality, the cross brought an end to their dreams and filled the disciples with despair. The Bible records, "Now from the sixth hour until the ninth hour there was darkness over all the land". And as dark as this was, the darkness of despair was darker than the darkness of the day. All their plans and dreams were ruined. All their hopes were dashed; there was nothing left, but the fearsome darkness of despair.

And yet, even in all this despair, the Bible tells us that Jesus, for the joy set before Him, endured the cross. The coming darkness of despair could not overwhelm Him, because He saw the joy that was to come. He saw the coming joy of the women coming to the tomb and finding that He was no longer bound there. He saw the coming joy of the disciples experiencing flashes of hope as they marveled to themselves about what had happened. He saw the coming joy of walking the road to Emmaus, expounding to the two disciples of things concerning what had and was about to happen and the joy when they understood. He saw the joy of meeting with the disciples and their great joy when they believed that He was alive; and the joy when even Thomas believed.

He saw the coming joy of the disciples meeting in Jerusalem as instructed and the Holy Spirit falling on them. And in that day when they were changed and the church was born. He saw the coming joy of millions of moments down through history, when men and women would come to know Him as Lord. Jesus saw the coming joy of His return as King of kings and Lord of lords. He saw the joy that was set before Him!

looking unto Jesus, the author and finisher of our faith,
who for the joy that was set before Him endured the cross,
despising the shame, and has sat down at the right hand
of the throne of God.

HEBREWS 12:2 (NKJV)

And I would be remiss if I did not ask about us as well. Jesus endured the cross, despising the shame. Jesus denied Himself and so we must do the same; discipleship costs. A disciple of Jesus dies daily, not a death of the body as Jesus experienced, but the death of ownership over their life. This is central to the Christian life and it is a key to success in a life of prayer.

Then Jesus said to His disciples, "If anyone desires to
come after Me, let him deny himself, and take up his
cross, and follow Me.

MATTHEW 16:24 (NKJV)

Paul told the Corinthians that he died daily. How did he die? He no longer had control over what he would do with his life. He was given fully to Jesus, the one he sought to be like, to follow obediently, and served wholeheartedly.

Dying daily to self is a cross we all must die upon. If we refuse to take up our cross and follow Jesus, then we limit our usefulness in prayer. If we hold on to the things of this world, pride, unforgiveness, selfishness, and the rest, we cannot pray effective prayers that avail much. The crucified life is a life purchased by God, a life we live for Him.

Derek Prince once described the crucified life, by asking three questions. First he asked, "Are you willing not to be in control?" The second question, "Are you willing to not be esteemed?" The third question, "Are you willing to not be secure?"

FOR THE JOY SET BEFORE HIM

Can you answer, yes, to these three questions? If we are to live the crucified life we must be fully and completely in God's hands.

Jesus endured for the joy that was set before Him. If we endure as he did, there is a great joy set before us as well. As we pray, we can see the coming joy of answers to prayers. We can see the coming joy of men and women won from death to life in Christ Jesus. We can see the coming joy of men and women delivered from bondage. We can see coming joy of nations turning from darkness to light. We can see the coming joy of hastening, the coming of the Kingdom of our Lord.

> *For what is our hope, or joy, or crown of rejoicing? Is it not even you in the presence of our Lord Jesus Christ at His coming? For you are our glory and joy.*
>
> I THESSALONIANS 2:19-20 (NKJV)

Let us pray!

Unit Three

COMPONENTS OF
EFFECTIVE PRAYER

The goodness of God is life altering. The goodness of God is a powerful key to walking in faith, power, and having an effective prayer life. We must not forget where we came from and where we are going; it is important to remember how different we are from, where we once were. This difference is due to the goodness of God. Beyond just remembering and reviewing the goodness of God, we also have a responsibility concerning the goodness of God. To those to whom much has been given, much is expected.

The goodness of God is an immeasurable blessing, and with this blessing comes responsibility. Very simply expressed, He wants us to be blessed, so we can be a blessing. We glorify God when we enjoy His goodness. Even more, we glorify God when we walk in our calling bringing His goodness to others.

Therefore we also pray always for you that our God
would count you worthy of this calling, and fulfill all the

good pleasure of His goodness and the work of faith with
power, that the name of our Lord Jesus Christ may be
glorified in you, and you in Him, according to the grace
of our God and the Lord Jesus Christ.

2 THESSALONIANS 1:11-12 (NKJV)

God is calling us to walk in our individual special assignment. Walking in our assignment, being faithful and full of faith, we please God. Walking in our assignment, brings the goodness of God to the world, walking our unique calling, brings glory to Him. This is especially true in prayer. God delights to bless us and answer our prayers. This is a wonderful part of the goodness of God.

Too often we have fallen short in our calling. We do some things; we try a little, but the day in which we live, needs men and women of prayer. We need the practice of effective prayer that brings the goodness of God to men and women's lives. This brings great glory to God.

Let us pray!

People talk about the value and blessing of effective prayer, which is good, there is nothing like prayer. If we are going to have success in prayer, we need to know and practice the basics. Unit Three, *Components of Effective Prayer* presents components of prayer, the foundation of our success.

BASICS OF EFFECTIVE PRAYER

Too often we get caught-up in the new and exciting, and we forget the basics. Prayer is so simple and we can have great success, if we will focus on and practice the basics. The basics of effective prayer include thanksgiving, humility, petition, and faith. So let us return to the basics.

Thanksgiving

Thanksgiving is very important to successful prayer. It should be present at the beginning and found throughout our prayers. Thanksgiving even helps us prepare for successful prayer, it changes our attitude. It is like turning on the light in a dark room. Thanksgiving reminds us of God's nature and abilities. And it is good to remember the wonderful things God has done for us and for others.

When we thank Him, we are changed, this gets us ready to ask God for answers to our needs, it gives us great confidence that God will answer. Generally, when we come to God in prayer it is because we need something and often are worried, fearful, lacking, hurting, stymied, or desperate. Thanksgiving will lift us from the pressure of these and help us to pray successfully.

Check your self, do you have a heart of thanksgiving? Does thanksgiving flavor what you say and do? And is this especially true in your prayers? Take time this week, yes, some of your prayer time, and just thank God. No requests, no begging, no complaints, no explaining, no anything, just thanks. This is an important secret to success in prayer; it will bring light and flavor to your life. Prayer with thanksgiving will revolutionize both your life and prayers! This week get back to the basics.

> *Be anxious for nothing, but in everything by prayer and supplication, with thanksgiving, let your requests be made known to God; and the peace of God, which surpasses all understanding, will guard your hearts and minds through Christ Jesus.*
>
> PHILIPPIANS 4:6-7 (NKJV)

> *Continue earnestly in prayer, being vigilant in it with thanksgiving;*
>
> COLOSSIANS 4:2 (NKJV)

Humility

Humility is a word that means not being proud. The humble person understands that God is the all powerful, all knowing God and we are his children. The humble person does not lean on his or her own skill, ability, or power, but leans on God, in all things. The humble person knows he or she needs God's help and needs answers to prayer, answers that come from God.

He has shown you, O man, what is good; And what does the Lord require of you But to do justly, To love mercy, And to walk humbly with your God?

MICAH 6:8 (NKJV)

But He gives more grace. Therefore He says: "God resists the proud, But gives grace to the humble." Therefore submit to God. Resist the devil and he will flee from you. Draw near to God and He will draw near to you. Cleanse your hands, you sinners; and purify your hearts, you double-minded. Lament and mourn and weep! Let your laughter be turned to mourning and your joy to gloom. Humble yourselves in the sight of the Lord, and He will lift you up.

JAMES 4:6-10 (NKJV)

Being humble is something we choose to do. We let God know we have needs and ask for answers. We believe that God is the one who can and will help us. We come to God in prayer and we come to God first, knowing we need His help in all we do. We seek Him, His will, and His answers to prayer; this is walking humbly with our God.

It is important that we do a self check and determine if we truly are humble. It is easy to make pretense of humility. For example, do we think we comprehend all we need to know to pray? A little knowledge can be dangerous and bring pride. Have we begun to lean on our prayer ability? Our flesh longs to be strong and in control, we need to be careful not to feed that longing, in prayer. God calls for us to humble our self in His sight.

A very effective way to learn humility is to fast. Fasting fights against attitudes and desires of the flesh. Fasting says no to the flesh. If we humble our self, putting under His control the flesh,

He will uplift us and our prayers. Basic number two is our attitude, are we humble? This week get back to the basics.

Petition or Request

This is more like what most people think of, when they talk about prayer, the request. This is one of the basics of effective prayer. Properly functioning in our life, it will bring success to our prayers.

There are several keys to making an effective request to God. For example, we need to make our request specific, telling God just what we need. When we ask people for things we make a specific request; why do we not follow this in prayer? One answer, of many, is that we are afraid to be specific, because then we, and others, will know if we receive answers. The answers are okay, but we fear not getting answers, so we hedge about and do not ask for specifics.

There are other factors to success in making a request. It is very powerful to ask first for answers for others. This is in compliance with the first commandment of God; love our neighbor. If we work to bless others, God will take care of our needs. We also need to request or ask in agreement with God's will. God likes to bless us, but He also protects us from things we should not have. Praying using Bible verses is the best way to know God's will on the matter.

There is more, when making a request in prayer, we must not doubt. We are commanded to believe and not to doubt, because doubt limits faith and our prayers. Another key is forgiveness, the requirement is to check and see if we have anything against anyone and deal with it. Forgiveness opens the door to answers. When we ask we should be specific, ask in love, ask in God's will, ask without doubting, and ask having forgiven. This week get back to the basics.

Now this is the confidence that we have in Him, that if we ask anything according to His will, He hears us. And if we know that He hears us, whatever we ask, we know that we have the petitions that we have asked of Him.

1 JOHN 5:14-15 (NKJV)

Faith

Faith is very important, it is required for effective prayer, and faith should be a part of each of the first three basics. Thanksgiving is by faith; we thank Him for the great things He has done, with confidence that He is still the great and powerful God. We also thank Him for the wonderful things we know He will do, this is by faith.

The humble person comes to God because they have faith; they know God is a faithful God and they can trust Him. He or she believes that the promises of God are good, that God is what He says He is (a great God who loves us and loves to do good things for us). They know He loves them and is working for them, not against them.

The petition or request should be in faith. We ask knowing that God is listening to our requests and God rewards those who come and ask Him in faith. Power in prayer is by faith manifest in thanksgiving, humility, and petition. This week get back to the basics.

So Jesus answered and said to them, "Assuredly, I say to you, if you have faith and do not doubt, you will not only do what was done to the fig tree, but also if you say to this mountain, 'Be removed and be cast into the sea,' it will be done. And whatever things you ask in prayer, believing, you will receive."

MATTHEW 21:21-22 (NKJV)

*If any of you lacks wisdom, let him ask of God, who gives
to all liberally and without reproach, and it will be given
to him. But let him ask in faith, with no doubting, for
he who doubts is like a wave of the sea driven and tossed
by the wind. For let not that man suppose that he will
receive anything from the Lord; he is a double-minded
man, unstable in all his ways.*

JAMES 1:5-8 (NKJV)

God is ready for us to be successful in life. He wants us
to win battles. To be successful in battle remember prayer. By
faith, humbly bring your request to God, with thanksgiving.
This week get back to the basics.

*Therefore I exhort first of all that supplications, prayers,
intercessions, and giving of thanks be made for all men,
for kings and all who are in authority, that we may lead
a quiet and peaceable life in all godliness and reverence.
For this is good and acceptable in the sight of God our
Savior, who desires all men to be saved and to come to the
knowledge of the truth.*

1 TIMOTHY 2:1-4 (NKJV)

Let us pray!

Article 17

STUDY GUIDE FOR EFFECTIVE PRAYER

Have you ever wondered about how many things there are to know? For a number of years I taught world history to high school students. Obviously this was a subject too big to learn in a school year, even if the students were interested in history. So I had study guides for each unit. These guides would help students focus on what I deemed to be important for them to learn. These were also guides to the material on the unit tests. Most of my students made use of these guides and this helped them be more successful learning history.

The subject of prayer is also very large. While prayer is so simple a child can do it, there is so much to learn that mastery of prayer can be and should be a life long pursuit. A question worth asking is what should we study?

It would be nice to have a study guide for effective prayer. The Bible provides several guides to praying effective prayers that we can use; the Lord's Prayer is one such guide. Millions of people have used this prayer as a guide or an outline to powerful prayers.

Paul also presents us with study guides. Paul is the man of faith, power, and evangelism; he is also the man of effective prayer. In the first chapter of Romans he shares information about his prayer life and in the process reveals some secrets to success in prayer. He deals with guarding the heart, practical practices, and building relationship with God and this makes for a good study on effective prayer.

> *For God is my witness, whom I serve with my spirit in the gospel of His Son, that without ceasing I make mention of you always in my prayers, making request if, by some means, now at last I may find a way in the will of God to come to you.*
>
> ROMANS 1:9-10 (NKJV)

This study guide can be very useful for the serious student of prayer. It can be of great value to review these points carefully and with the help of the Holy Spirit apply them to our prayer life. He is willing and able to help us to measure our understanding, and more importantly, to measure our current practices, and learn to pray effective prayers.

Point One – God is My Witness

A witness is one who has personal knowledge of something. Does God have personal knowledge of you and your prayers? The answer is of course He does, He is God and knows everything. However, the key here is does He have personal knowledge because you and He have a close, ongoing relationship in prayer?

There are many things that go into it, but effective prayer begins with and must remain firmly established in the relationship. Effective prayer is a relationship with God. Jesus' power in prayer came from His relationship with the Father. We must work to have a close relationship with Him. We need to be one with the Father just as Jesus was and is today. Can God witness today of your close relationship, a relationship of Father, Jesus, and the Holy Spirit with their cherished son or daughter; that is with you?

> *I do not pray for these alone, but also for those who will believe in Me through their word; that they all may be one, as You, Father, are in Me, and I in You; that they also may be one in Us, that the world may believe that You sent Me. And the glory which You gave Me I have given them, that they may be one just as We are one:*
>
> JOHN 17:20-22 (NKJV)

Point Two – Whom I Serve

The call to effective prayer is a call to service. There are people who pray because they are desperate for answers, or face seemingly impossible situations. However, a prayer life, especially an effective prayer life, one that avails much, comes from a servant's heart. Jesus stated that He came to serve. Paul claimed to be a servant. And we must, if we are to have success, be servants, as well.

Effective prayer takes up the yoke of Jesus; joining with Him to carry a burden for the lost. The Father's heart cry is to the lost whom He loves. Our service will vary in our specific work, but our motivation will be, winning the lost. If we are not willing to be a servant, then we limit our success in prayer. And a note for advanced students, or those longing to be advanced; a servant does not get to pick where and how he will serve, he serves at the command of the Father.

All things have been delivered to Me by My Father, and no one knows the Son except the Father. Nor does anyone know the Father except the Son, and the one to whom the Son wills to reveal Him. Come to Me, all you who labor and are heavy laden, and I will give you rest. Take My yoke upon you and learn from Me, for I am gentle and lowly in heart, and you will find rest for your souls. For My yoke is easy and My burden is light."

MATTHEW 11:27-30 (NKJV)

Point Three – With My Spirit

Prayer is not just physical, nor is it just words, it must be spiritual. We cannot have effective prayer if we are not praying in the spirit. God is spirit and those that come to Him must come in sprit and truth.

However, when He, the Spirit of truth, has come, He will guide you into all truth; for He will not speak on His own authority, but whatever He hears He will speak; and He will tell you things to come.

JOHN 16:13 (NKJV)

Point Four – In the Gospel of His Son

A central theme of our prayers should be the proclamation of the Gospel of Jesus Christ. We have been crucified with Christ and we do not have a life of our own, it is Christ who lives in us. Our life, service, work, and everything else, is to be a part of spreading the Gospel message. Our prayers and the answers to these prayers are for bringing the Gospel message to people and helping people receive and living in its blessing.

And He said to them, "Go into all the world and preach the gospel to every creature. He who believes and is

baptized will be saved; but he who does not believe will
be condemned.

MARK 16:15-16 (NKJV)

Point Five – Without Ceasing

Without ceasing is a command for prayer as a normal practice and it is to be practiced without exception. God has called us to pray for people, situations, and nations and if we are going to be faithful to this call we must not let anything keep us from our appointed duties.

There are many ways we can be kept from prayer. First there are the physical ways, things that are trying to interrupt our prayer time. An example of this concern for prayer without ceasing is taken from the book *Power through Prayer* by E. M. Bounds.

> "A desire for God which cannot break the chains of sleep
> is a weak thing and will do but little good for God after
> it has indulged itself fully. The desire for God that keeps
> so far behind the devil and the world at the beginning of
> the day will never catch up".

There are also spiritual ways to keep us from effective prayer. The Devil does not want prayer, but he is especially concerned about effective, fervent prayer. To keep us from prayer is appealing to him, but if that is not possible, then to keep us from praying in faith is the next best thing. To be effective we must pray in faith. Here is a good question for us to regularly review, "Is it my practice to faithfully pray, and pray in faith, everyday?"

Point Six – Mention

Effective prayer is spoken prayer. Faith is an act and if we are to pray effectively, we must act on our faith. This begins

105

with our words and continues with our actions. It is easy to have negative thoughts that cloud our prayers and hinder our faith. The best way to clear these clouds away is to speak out our prayers of faith.

By speaking we tame our thinking. No longer do we allow negative, faith dampening thoughts to reside in our mind. This of course is assuming you do not speak negative words when you pray. David knew the importance of what he said and asked God to put a guard over his mouth so he would not say negative, faith killing things. What do you have to say in prayer? Please note, it is also very important that we watch what we say when we are not praying.

> *Set a guard, O Lord, over my mouth; Keep watch over the door of my lips.*
>
> PSALM 141:3 (NKJV)

Point Seven – Always

If we are seeking to be effective in prayer, we will face times when the answers seem like they will never come. When we face these times, we must continue in faith. Prayer is by faith and commitment and we can not falter and stop.

Part of Paul's great success was so simple anyone can see it, he always prayed. Nothing would stop him, nothing could hinder him. He was fully persuaded that God was faithful and so he knew he would have answers. Do you always pray and always praying in faith?

Point Eight – Making Request

In a relationship between a son and father there are different roles for each. The father provides for the needs of the son, including: security, provision, guidance, direction, encouragement, love, and much more. The son's role is to love the father, to honor him, and to learn from him. The faithful son will ask of his father, knowing that the father delights to give to the son. Our Heavenly Father delights to give to His sons and daughters. He delights to give answers to their prayers.

So a part of our relationship with our Father is asking and receiving. We must confidently come to Him and ask, knowing that He delights to give answers and to bless us. He wants us to be blessed, so we can be a blessing. Have you been a good son or daughter; have you been asking?

> *Now this is the confidence that we have in Him, that if we ask anything according to His will, He hears us. And if we know that He hears us, whatever we ask, we know that we have the petitions that we have asked of Him.*
>
> I JOHN 5:14-15 (NKJV)

Point Nine – Find a Way in the Will of God

The will of God is an important key to success in prayer. God has made bold promises concerning His willingness and ability to answer prayer, when we pray, in His will. When we yield our will and seek first and foremost His will, there is no limit to the answers we can receive in prayer. We draw close to God and tune our ear to hear His voice, listen carefully, and then obey what He says. Please note, a great way to know the will of God, is searching the Bible. God has placed His will in His Word. Effective prayer finds the will of God and makes it of chief importance, and proceeds by speaking and acting in faith.

So there you have it, a quick study guide for effective prayer. If we study and apply these points concerning prayer, we can be very successful in prayer. How about you, will you be a good student. Will you study the points of the guide and apply them to your prayer life? Will you seeking to be close to the Father, faithful in practice, and effective in prayer?

> *The effective, fervent prayer of a righteous man avails much.*
>
> JAMES 5:16 (NKJV)

Let us pray!

COMPONENTS OF EFFECTIVE PRAYER

When I was stationed in Germany, the military worked hard to make things nice for the GIs. We had special stores we could use and one of the best was shopping in the stereo store. In this store, manufacturers of stereo equipment displayed their new equipment. We had access to all of the best stereo components and we could buy at reduced prices and so many rooms in the barracks, had great stereo systems with wonderful components.

In my family there has been a tradition of great cooks. Each cook could produce a great meal and each had specialties, items everyone asked for. One often asked for item was and is pie. All the cooks made, and many still make, great pies, with light, flaky crust. The ingredients for a pie crust are very simple; success in making a great crust is how you use those ingredients.

Great things come from great parts. A great stereo or a great pie crust, the first requirement for a great outcome is the components. Great components make the system great. A component is the constituent (the essential) parts, the ingredients. The result is only as good as the parts and how they are acted upon. A stereo cannot produce great music if it has poor speakers. Pie crust is simple, but what you do with the ingredients can make for a crust people rave about.

This is true with prayer as well. Prayer is made of several components. With all the components in place, prayer can be very powerful. With missing components, our prayers are hindered. With the components in place, we can still miss the mark of the high calling of God for prayer, if we do not handle the components well. If we are going to be effective in prayer we must have both, the components of prayer and use them as God directs.

If we are interested in success in prayer, and having a powerful prayer life, then it would be good for us to review components of effective prayer and their proper use. Take a moment and see if these components are a consistent part of your prayer life and if you use them well.

Specific Request

Our first component is to make a specific request. We need to ask what we desire God to do or what we want from Him. A specific request is precise, detailed, and definite. It trusts God to hear our prayer and give an answer. Even though He knows what we need, it is His divine plan that we come to Him and make known our wants.

This seems simple and straightforward, but it can be a problem for people. If we are specific about our requests, then there is a measuring rod for determining our effectiveness. If we do not have confidence in God or our faith, this can be scary; with specific requests we will see if we have gotten answers to our prayers. Too often people opt out of this pressure by just praying general prayers, they are not sure they will get answers and they do not want to look bad if they fail. This is unfortunate for them, they miss a great opportunity. A component of effective prayer is the specific request. We must have faith in God to answer and with faith in God we can be bold to make specific requests.

> *But let him ask in faith, with no doubting, for he who doubts is like a wave of the sea driven and tossed by the wind. For let not that man suppose that he will receive anything from the Lord; he is a double-minded man, unstable in all his ways.*
>
> JAMES 1:6-8 (NKJV)

Scripture Based

A second component is establishing our prayers on the Word of God. Prayer is more effective if we are praying in the will of God and a great way to know His will is to find out what He says in the Bible. Search the Bible for scriptures that apply to the current need and then pray using these verses. This builds a foundation for our faith and great confidence in prayer.

The key is to read and meditate on these Scriptures, until they are firmly planted in our heart and they have built our faith. The amount of the Word we need in our heart for successful prayer is what it takes for abundance. Abundance of the Word is when it overflows out of our heart. With abundance we can have faith. With abundance we are prepared to stand against attacks of Satan.

> *This Book of the Law shall not depart from your mouth, but you shall meditate in it day and night, that you may observe to do according to all that is written in it. For*

then you will make your way prosperous, and then you
will have good success.

JOSHUA 1:8 (NKJV)

Believe that You Receive

Prayer is by faith. We must believe that God hears and answers prayers. People are willing to believe what they can see and feel, but sometimes it is hard to believe in the things of the spirit world. If we are going to be effective in prayer we must come to recognize that there is a spirit realm and things of that realm are made real in the natural realm through faith.

This goes beyond our natural thinking and can be difficult. However, we are told to walk by faith and not by sight. In the natural, circumstances seem very real, but by faith they can be changed. A stubborn faith that refuses to be limited by circumstances produces results in prayer. If we believe, we can receive answers when we pray, we will receive answers.

> *For assuredly, I say to you, whoever says to this mountain,*
> *'Be removed and be cast into the sea,' and does not doubt*
> *in his heart, but believes that those things he says will be*
> *done, he will have whatever he says. Therefore I say to*
> *you, whatever things you ask when you pray, believe that*
> *you receive them, and you will have them.*

MARK 11:23-24 (NKJV)

> *Blessed be the God and Father of our Lord Jesus Christ,*
> *who has blessed us with every spiritual blessing in the*
> *heavenly places in Christ,*

EPHESIANS 1:3 (NKJV)

> *Now this is the confidence that we have in Him, that if*
> *we ask anything according to His will, He hears us. And*

112

if we know that He hears us, whatever we ask, we know
that we have the petitions that we have asked of Him.

1 JOHN 5:14-15 (NKJV)

There are more components to effective prayer, but this is a good start for this article. The challenge is what we will do with these components. Remember our pie crust. The ingredients are simple and well know to everyone, but the key to great flaky crust is how you use the ingredients. It is one thing to know these ingredients of effective prayer; we must also check our actions and use them well.

Faith Comes

Using the components of effective prayer requires first and foremost, faith. We must operate in all the components of prayer by faith. The great news is that faith comes. It comes by the Word of God (Romans 10:17).

We need to be spending time in the Word of God, building our faith. Our time should include our daily devotions. In addition, we need time reading, studying, meditating, and acting on specific promises of the Word of God that apply to areas of our prayer needs. If we will diligently spend time in the Word and allow it to train us and prepare us, we can apply the Word to our life and prayers, and our faith will be active and powerful.

Watch Your Mouth

A second key to successfully using the components of effective prayer is watching what we say. When we pray we want to be careful what we say; we should agree with God. A bigger problem is watching what we say, when we are not praying. It is easy to slip into speaking doubt, fear, and unbelief. We need to join with King David and ask for help with our mouth. Tame your mouth and you can have great success in prayer.

> *Set a guard, O Lord, over my mouth; Keep watch over the door of my lips.*
>
> PSALM 141:3 (NKJV)

Just Do It!

Finally, for this list, we need to check on our actions. It is one thing to know about the components of prayer, but to be successful we must be active doers of the Word. What is your track record, are you just watching from the sidelines or are you a doer of the Word? Put these components together and use them as God directs and we can be effective in prayer.

> *But be doers of the word, and not hearers only, deceiving yourselves.*
>
> JAMES 1:22 (NKJV)

Let us pray!

POWER IN PRAYER

I like trains. I have enjoyed them since I was a boy and my dad brought home a model train for Christmas. I love the way they look and sound. I like models and the real thing and with real trains I love the power. The sight and sound, and oh yes the feel, of a great engine pulling cars loaded with tons and tons of goods, now that is exciting.

Near our house there is a track and several freight trains run there every day. Sometimes they come up through town and then stop by the park were I walk. They then reverse their direction and go back to pick up or drop off cars. When these huge engines are sitting there not moving, but are full of pent up power, you hear and feel the immense power. The engineer gives a blast of his whistle, releases the brakes, and the train, begins to move again. That is power!

We live in an age of power; everywhere we look we see great power. The mightiest power of all these powers is the power of prayer. Prayer can move mountains, turn nations, and touch hearts. However, to often this great power is pent up, waiting to be released, and this requires many components; each to be operational in our life.

The previous article from *Voice of Thanksgiving*, studied some components of prayer. These components were related to the task of asking, making a petition to God. These components were specific request, scripture based, and believing that you receive. There was also mentioned some practices for making the components of petition work; faith, guarding our mouth, and being doers of the Word. In this article we focus on components of power in prayer.

Component #1 – Dealing with Faith Destroying Forces: Doubt, Fear, and Unbelief

There are forces; doubt, fear, and unbelief, operating in the world trying to destroy faith. The antidote for these faith destroyers is the Word of God. The application here is the filling of our heart with the Word of God, full to overflowing. Many people read their Bibles and they expect this to be enough. The problem is, they are just dipping their toe in the Word and they need to be fully submerged in the Word, they need to be in over their head.

Effective faith is always being in over our head; faith requires diving into God and His Word without reserve. It takes more than just casual reading of the Bible to overcome the power of doubt, fear, and unbelief. The Word in abundance in your heart will come pouring out of your mouth. You are going to talk, the question is what you will say; your words spoken in faith; will produce life, healing, and prosperity, and they will produce effective prayers.

> *My son, give attention to my words; Incline your ear to my sayings. Do not let them depart from your eyes; Keep them in the midst of your heart; For they are life to those*

*who find them, And health to all their flesh. Keep your
heart with all diligence, For out of it spring the issues
of life. Put away from you a deceitful mouth, And put
perverse lips far from you.*

PROVERBS 4:20-24 (NKJV)

*Death and life are in the power of the tongue, And those
who love it will eat its fruit.*

PROVERBS 18:21 (NKJV)

*Brood of vipers! How can you, being evil, speak good
things? For out of the abundance of the heart the mouth
speaks. A good man out of the good treasure of his heart
brings forth good things, and an evil man out of the evil
treasure brings forth evil things. But I say to you that for
every idle word men may speak, they will give account of
it in the day of judgment. For by your words you will be
justified, and by your words you will be condemned.*

MATTHEW 12:34-37 (NKJV)

The key is to make good choices and act on them. Doubt, fear, and unbelief are choices. They are not given to us by God. We can choose to walk in these faith destroying activities or we can believe the promises of God. By studying the Bible, concentrating on the promises of God, we can come to believe God over any other evidence. This is what Abraham did and God called him a man of faith. We can do the same thing; meditate on the promises of God until they become more real than the problems we face. Faith that knows God, His promises, and His abilities, will believe Him and in Him, and will be bold in prayer.

And not being weak in faith, he did not consider his own body, already dead (since he was about a hundred years old), and the deadness of Sarah's womb. He did not waver at the promise of God through unbelief, but was strengthened in faith, giving glory to God, and being fully convinced that what He had promised He was also able to perform.

ROMANS 4:19-21 (NKJV)

So Jesus answered and said to them, "Have faith in God. For assuredly, I say to you, whoever says to this mountain, 'Be removed and be cast into the sea,' and does not doubt in his heart, but believes that those things he says will be done, he will have whatever he says. Therefore I say to you, whatever things you ask when you pray, believe that you receive them, and you will have them.

MARK 11:22-24 (NKJV)

Component #2 - Authority in the Name of Jesus

Jesus teaches us that we are to pray to the Father. This is a privilege afforded to the Father's sons and daughters. This access to the Father, won by Jesus on the Cross, is a legal right of the born again children of God. This access gives us great power in prayer. We have His promise that if we come to Him, He will listen, hear, and answer our prayer!

Let us therefore come boldly to the throne of grace, that we may obtain mercy and find grace to help in time of need.

HEBREWS 4:16 (NKJV)

Jesus also teaches us that when we pray we are to use His name. There is great power in the name of Jesus and we have been authorized to use His name in prayer. It is like having his power of attorney when we pray. A power of attorney is authorization to act as the agent for another person. Jesus is giving us the right to use His name; this is permitting us to act for Him when we pray. To pray effectively in the name of Jesus we must be Born Again, the use of His name is reserved for His children. We must know what He wants us to do, so we need to spend time with Him and in His Word. This gives us the foundation for our faith, boldness, and power in prayer.

> *And in that day you will ask Me nothing. Most assuredly, I say to you, whatever you ask the Father in My name He will give you. Until now you have asked nothing in My name. Ask, and you will receive, that your joy may be full.*
>
> JOHN 16:23-24 (NKJV)

> *Now this is the confidence that we have in Him, that if we ask anything according to His will, He hears us. And if we know that He hears us, whatever we ask, we know that we have the petitions that we have asked of Him.*
>
> I JOHN 5:14-15 (NKJV)

Component #3 - Standing Firm

God has done great things for us. He has prepared the way for us to pray and has made terrific promises about answering our prayers. His requirement is that in all we do, walk, talk, act, and pray, all must be by faith. Without faith we cannot please Him, nor can we live a successful Christian life or have effective prayers. We know God's ground rules, He requires faith. The problem is that walking by faith can be difficult at times.

Throughout the Bible, God presents a call to stand firm on His plan, promises, and provision. Effectiveness comes to the man or woman who will stand, and more specific, stand consistently. A flash of faith now and then is better than none, but effective prayer and a victorious Christian living, requires a consistent walk in faith. If we are going to have powerful prayers, we must discipline our life to consistently stand in faith and firmly stand on God's promises. God is faithful, what He has said, He will do, but He wants us to be consistent as well. The consistently faithful will have power in prayer.

> *that we should no longer be children, tossed to and fro and carried about with every wind of doctrine, by the trickery of men, in the cunning craftiness of deceitful plotting,*
>
> EPHESIANS 4:14 (NKJV)

> *For we have become partakers of Christ if we hold the beginning of our confidence steadfast to the end,*
>
> HEBREWS 3:14 (NKJV)

> *Let us hold fast the confession of our hope without wavering, for He who promised is faithful.*
>
> HEBREWS 10:23 (NKJV)

> *For you have need of endurance, so that after you have done the will of God, you may receive the promise:*
>
> HEBREWS 10:36 (NKJV)

> *And you, who once were alienated and enemies in your mind by wicked works, yet now He has reconciled in the body of His flesh through death, to present you holy, and blameless, and above reproach in His sight-- if indeed you continue in the faith, grounded and steadfast, and are not moved away from the hope of the gospel which*

you heard, which was preached to every creature under
heaven, of which I, Paul, became a minister.

COLOSSIANS 1:21-23 (NKJV)

These are a few of the components of power in prayer, deal with faith destroyers, pray with the authority of Jesus' name, and standing firm and consistent. Faithfully applied to our life and prayers, they will yield great power in prayer. There are more components, others we need to explore and apply to our life, but they will have to wait for the next time.

Let us pray!

BLESSED BACK

Happy Birthday! Simple words that mean a lot, but one time they were extra special. The first year I was in the military, I was sent to Germany. It was hard to be away from my family and to make things worse, at that time it was expensive to make calls overseas, so I very rarely called home. However, I decided to make arrangements to make a surprise call to my Mom on her birthday. I wrote to my friend Mark and asked him to contact my Dad. The plan was to set up for Mom to be home at a certain time on her birthday and I would call. Mark and my Dad got everything arranged.

Making phone calls in those days was not just expensive, but took some effort. On my Mom's birthday, I went to the German Bundestpost; this is the post office and telephone exchange all in one. This was where GIs and others would go to make personal overseas calls. When I got there, I had a big surprise. They were just closing for the night. I had assumed they were open 24-7. All I could think of was everyone at home waiting for a call, a call that never came.

I talked with the man who was closing, explaining what I wanted to do, his English was very good, and he said he would stay open for my call. He setup the call and it went through. My brother Bill answered and I told him to get Mom. In a few seconds she answered and I got to say, "Happy Birthday!"

Communications have come a long way. Phone calls were difficult then, today we carry phones and can call anywhere in the world at any time. One time while I was in Poland at a conference, I had some free time, so I went to a nearby park. I thought I should call someone to make sure that my cell phone was working. So I called my Mom. No set up or plans were needed, just call. I just entered a few numbers, the phone rang, and I was talking to my Mom.

With computers, communication is faster than ever. We have a subscriber to *Voice of Thanksgiving* who lives in Asia. This man has setup his email to send a message letting you know when he is out of the office. One night I sent out *Voice of Thanksgiving* and before I could check to see if my emails had gone through, I got this message back from him.

In the last few articles we have been studying components of effective prayer. It is important to regularly review the basic components and check for obedience to God's Word and consistency in our practices. It is easy to assume knowledge and good practices, but sometimes we slip into mistakes or omissions. The components in the last article were Component #1 - Dealing with Faith Destroying Forces – Doubt, Fear, and Unbelief, Component #2 - Authority in the Name of Jesus, and Component #3 - Standing Firm.

The components this week should play a central role in our prayer life and daily practices. These components also come with a blessing beyond answers to prayer. When we pray with these components, God sends a blessing back to us. Like the email message of notification for being out of the office returned to me, these give an immediate blessing. Answers to prayer and a blessing, now that is a good deal!

Component #4 - Praise and Thanksgiving

Praise and thanksgiving should be central to all our prayers. They are actually both a form of prayer and a component of power, in other forms of prayer. Praise is offered to God for who He is and what He has done in general. Thanksgiving is offered to God for what He has done for us in particular. If we come with difficulties and troubles on our mind, praise and thanksgiving, can change us and position us to receive answers.

> *Be anxious for nothing, but in everything by prayer and supplication, with thanksgiving, let your requests be made known to God;*
>
> PHILIPPIANS 4:6 (NKJV)

> *Enter into His gates with thanksgiving, And into His courts with praise. Be thankful to Him, and bless His name.*
>
> PSALM 100:4 (NKJV)

Praise and thanksgiving give us direct access to God. The gates lead into His courts, the courts lead into His presence. You get through the gates with thanksgiving and through the courts with praise. In His presence is fullness of joy and answered prayers.

Praise and thanksgiving is a great way to open our prayer times and they should be a central part throughout. Faith is required for successful prayer; and praise and thanksgiving encourages and expresses our faith. Prayer with thanksgiving and praise is giving thanks before something happens. This is a great demonstration of faith.

> *Be anxious for nothing, but in everything by prayer and supplication, with thanksgiving, let your requests be made known to God; and the peace of God, which surpasses all understanding, will guard your hearts and minds through Christ Jesus.*
>
> PHILIPPIANS 4:6-7 (NKJV)

Component #5 – Praying in the Holy Spirit, the Release of Power

> *For as many as are led by the Spirit of God, these are sons of God.*
>
> ROMANS 8:14 (NKJV)

This is the continuing present tense in the Greek, so we can read it as, "As many as are regularly led by the Spirit of God, they are the sons of God". This is being regularly, continually led by the Holy Spirit. Paul, later in this same chapter, applies this leading of the Holy Spirit to prayer.

> *Likewise the Spirit also helps in our weaknesses. For we do not know what we should pray for as we ought, but the Spirit Himself makes intercession for us with groanings which cannot be uttered. Now He who searches the hearts knows what the mind of the Spirit is, because He makes intercession for the saints according to the will of God.*
>
> ROMANS 8:26-27 (NKJV)

The Spirit helps us in our weaknesses. For example, we often do not know what we should pray. Derek Prince expresses Paul's lament as:

"We do not know what to pray for as we ought. Or to state it another way, we do not always know what to pray for, and even if we do, many times we still do not know how to pray for it. You might know that your son needs prayer or your friend needs prayer, but you still do not know how to pray"

From *Secrets of a Prayer Warrior* by Derek Prince

However, God has given us help so we can pray effectively; He has given the Holy Spirit to help us. We can and should let Him pray through us. When we pray in unknown tongues, praying in the Spirit, we are praying the prayer He wants prayed, praying according to God's will. We do the talking, but the Holy Spirit gives us the words to say. The direction to our speaking comes from the Holy Spirit, to our spirit, instead of from our mind. We do the praying, the Holy Spirit helps us to pray Spirit-directed prayers. This makes for very powerful and effective praying.

> *praying always with all prayer and supplication in the Spirit, being watchful to this end with all perseverance and supplication for all the saints—*
>
> EPHESIANS 6:18 (NKJV)

> *For if I pray in a tongue, my spirit prays, but my understanding is unfruitful.*
>
> I CORINTHIANS 14:14 (NKJV)

> *"My spirit (by the Holy Spirit within me) prays."*
>
> I CORINTHIANS 14:14 (AMPLIFIED VERSION)

Both of these components are central to powerful prayers. They help us to pray effective prayers that avail much. They should be in the arsenal of everyone seeking power in prayer and they come with a direct blessing from God.

Praise and thanksgiving must have first place, regular place, and final place in prayer. Giving thanks has a very important psychological function. It builds our faith. The more we stop and thank God for all He has done for us, the easier it is for us to believe that He is going to do what we ask next.

And a life of prayer without praying in the Holy Spirit is like fighting a huge fire with a bucket, when a fire hose is available for our use. Praying in the Spirit also helps us to learn more fully to trust God and keeps worldly ideas from our prayers. It also comes with an extra blessing, praying in the Holy Spirit gives us a spiritual refreshing. Praying in tongues is an exercise of faith in God and the Holy Spirit and it helps edify the believer.

> *For with stammering lips and another tongue He will speak to this people, To whom He said, "This is the rest with which You may cause the weary to rest," And, "This is the refreshing"; Yet they would not hear.*
>
> ISAIAH 28:11-12 (NKJV)

> *But you, beloved, building yourselves up on your most holy faith, praying in the Holy Spirit,*
>
> JUDE 1:20 (NKJV)

Let us pray!

THE CORRECT PRAYER
FOR THE JOB

There is a cartoon that I have always enjoyed, I first saw it 30 or 40 years ago, but I still enjoy it when I see it or think of it. It shows a workman nailing up a sign, the sign says, "Workers must use the correct tool for the job". He is nailing up the sign with a wrench.

The cartoon rings true because we have all done things like this. Many falls and injuries come from the use of something other than the correct tool. And using the wrong tool can be more than just dangerous, but also make the job more difficult.

This battle to have and use the correct tool for the job carries over into the realm of prayer. There are various types of prayer and we should use the correct type for the situation we face. The rules for one type are different from the rules for another. Knowing how to pray and seeking to be effective in prayer demands that we know the types of prayer and use the correct prayer for the job.

The last few weeks we have been studying components of effective prayer. Today we will continue; the focus is on several main types of prayer and their proper use. Effective prayer demands faith and we cannot be successful without faith, but it also demands we pray as directed by our Father.

Component #6 – The Correct Prayer for the Job

Some people say prayer is prayer and it does not matter, but far too often these people get poor, if any, results. If we are interested in effective prayer, we need to understand and properly practice the use of the prayer of petition, prayer of praise and thanksgiving, prayer of commitment, and intercession.

Prayer of Petition

What most people think of when they think of prayer is the prayer of petition; asking God for an answer to deal with a need. This ranges from a cry of desperation to a presentation of a formal request. The prayer of petition has guidelines of best practice.

Effective prayer of petition requires faith, which is required of all types of prayer. Next we need to build a close relationship with the Father, abiding with Him and guarding our heart. God has presented His will in the Bible. Taking time to search out verses that apply to the subject of our prayers, helps build our faith, causes us to think correctly; it gives focus to our thinking, and confidence to pray. Knowing God's will on the subject is very helpful. A petition presented to the Father with His words and promises, followed by a stand of faith, will see God change situations and bring the answers we need.

Now this is the confidence that we have in Him, that if
we ask anything according to His will, He hears us. And

if we know that He hears us, whatever we ask, we know that we have the petitions that we have asked of Him.

I JOHN 5:14-15 (NKJV)

Prayer of Praise and Thanksgiving

Praise and thanksgiving give us direct access to God. They are a great way to open our prayer times and should play an important part throughout our prayer. Faith is required for successful prayer, and praise and thanksgiving encourage and express our faith. Praise is offered to God for who He is and what He has done in general. Thanksgiving is offered to God for what He has done for us in particular.

Enter into His gates with thanksgiving, And into His courts with praise. Be thankful to Him, and bless His name.

PSALM 100:4 (NKJV)

Be anxious for nothing, but in everything by prayer and supplication, with thanksgiving, let your requests be made known to God; and the peace of God, which surpasses all understanding, will guard your hearts and minds through Christ Jesus.

PHILIPPIANS 4:6-7 (NKJV)

Prayer of Commitment

The prayer of commitment or dedication is praying God's will for your life. This is used in a variety of applications, but the most common is seeking God's will for our work or ministry. This prayer would be used, for example, when offering to serve in a mission field or ministry. It is used when seeking to know how and where God would like for you to serve. This is a surrender of my will and seeking to do God's will. The question associated with this type of prayer is, what does God want me do with my life? The greatest example of this is Jesus in the Garden of Gethsemane.

> *He went a little farther and fell on His face, and prayed, saying, "O My Father, if it is possible, let this cup pass from Me; nevertheless, not as I will, but as You will."*
>
> MATTHEW 26:39 (NKJV)

Prayer of commitment is the place where it is appropriate to use the phrase, "if it be Thy will". In the prayer of petition we are praying from a position of knowing the will of God. For example, we already know God's will on healing. He desires that we be healed and walk in health. We already know God's will on finances; my God shall supply all my need. In the prayer of praise and thanksgiving we know the nature and abilities of God, this is what we are praising, and by faith, thanking Him for. In the intercession (the next type of prayer) we know the gap where we must stand and seek God's mercy. In the prayer of commitment, we are seeking something we do not know; we are seeking God's will for our life.

Intercession

Our fourth type of prayer, intercession, is very powerful and it often requires practice to be effective. The intercessor is one who stands before God for those for whom he is praying. We have well know examples from the Bible; Abraham for the city of Sodom and Moses for the Jewish people in the desert. Read this account from the book of Psalms about Moses and this intercession.

> *They made a calf in Horeb, And worshiped the molded image. Thus they changed their glory Into the image of an ox that eats grass. They forgot God their Savior, Who*

had done great things in Egypt, Wondrous works in the land of Ham, Awesome things by the Red Sea. Therefore He said that He would destroy them, Had not Moses His chosen one stood before Him in the breach, To turn away His wrath, lest He destroy them.

PSALM 106:19-23 (NKJV)

This is a wonderful picture of an intercessor. When someone's sin has caused a gap, the intercessor stands in the breach for that person. Intercession is carried out for individuals, groups, or nations. The intercessor cries out to God for mercy.

Intercession is most often a hidden life, far from the limelight of the world. It is like the life of Anna recorded in Luke chapter two. She lived her life as an intercessor, always in prayer and fasting. She was there crying out for Israel and for their redemption. She was rewarded for her years of prayer by seeing the Redeemer and recognizing Him.

Derek Prince presents four qualifications for us if we wish to be an intercessor.

"First of all, an intercessor must have an absolute conviction of God's righteousness, but he must be absolutely convinced also that God will judge the wicked. Second, he has to have a deep concern for God's glory. Third, I believe such a person must have an intimate acquaintance with God. An intercessor is a person who can stand before God and talk to Him with the utmost frankness—and yet reverence. And finally, to be an intercessor takes holy boldness. You must be willing to risk your life. As an intercessor you say, "I may run the risk of death, but I am going to stand here.""

From *Secrets of a Prayer Warrior* by Derek Prince

I have set watchmen on your walls, O Jerusalem; They shall never hold their peace day or night. You who make mention of the Lord, do not keep silent, And give Him no rest till He establishes And till He makes Jerusalem a praise in the earth.

ISAIAH 62:6-7 (NKJV)

Effective prayer is worth working for. God has made provision for us, opening the way for us to come boldly into His throne room. He has made remarkable promises and stands by His Word. Success in prayer comes by faithful application of the proper prayer for the situation.

Let us prays!

Unit Four

WALKING IN EFFECTIVE PRAYER

Sometimes a story makes things easier to understand and remember. We can relate to the people and events in a story which makes it easier for us to apply the principles of the story. We use this method with children all the time. Parents have read stories to their children for hundreds of years and used the stories as a teaching tool. So, today I would like to tell you two stories, one from the Bible and one more contemporary. They are both simple stories and many of you will know one or both stories. In both stories the people prayed and God does awesome things.

The first story is from the Bible and involves a King with a catchy name, Jehoshaphat. Jehoshaphat was the fourth king to rule Judah after the split of the kingdom. He was 35 when he became king and ruled for 25 years. One day Jehoshaphat and the people of Judah found out that a mighty army was coming to try to conquer them. The army was so big it was called a multitude. There seemed to be no way they could defeat this army, so Jehoshaphat and all the people were afraid. In desperation Jehoshaphat declared they would seek the Lord's help, so they fasted and prayed. God heard their prayers and answered.

> *You will not need to fight in this battle. Position yourselves, stand still and see the salvation of the Lord, who is with you, O Judah and Jerusalem!' Do not fear or be dismayed; tomorrow go out against them, for the Lord is with you.*
>
> 2 CHRONICLES 20:17 (NKJV)

So the people did what God said to do. They saw God do what He said He would do and it was amazing. God caused the army coming against them to kill themselves. The army left so much stuff behind, it took three days to collect all the spoils.

And now the second story; in 1920 Rees Howells saw a need for a Christian training college and God sent him to an area near Swansea, Wales. As he prayed, God guided him to a large estate named Glynderwen. Rees was convinced that this is where God wanted to place the college.

At this time Rees had about 2 shillings and he soon found out that the estate would cost more than £6000 (At that time there was 20 shillings to a Pound). And there were other groups, backed with plenty of money, that were bidding to buy the estate. Rees had never been involved in buying something this expensive. He did not have a church, denomination, group or benefactor behind him to help. In the natural Rees buying this estate seemed impossible.

Impossible or not, Rees began to pray and believe God for the purchase. The process lasted months. There were deposits that had to be paid and often Rees did not have the money, even the day before the deadline. However, step-by-step each obstacle was overcome and Rees purchased the estate and established the Bible College of Wales.

These two stories are examples of effective prayer. While most of us are not facing a massive army bearing down on us, with our destruction in mind or massive costs to complete a God given project, we do face difficult times and situations. What we need is effective prayer, because effective prayer is, effective.

Effective prayer is praying for a definite object. When we pray we must focus on one thing and seek it fully. All of the examples from the Bible of effective prayer are focused on one point of need. Wherever we see the blessing, sought for in prayer, attained, we find that the prayer offered was prayer for a definite object.

Effective prayer is persevering prayer. Most prayer is presented and forgotten. This is why many people must go back to God many times with the same request. They do not pray in faith and even if they do, they do not continue in faith until the answer comes.

Effective prayer is offered in the name of Jesus. There is no other name filled with the power for answers. The Bible direction is that we pray to the Father, and that these prayers should be in Jesus' name.

Effective prayer is aided, guided, and empowered by the Holy Spirit. In our own strength we cannot pray effective prayers. We must pray by faith and we must have the hand of the Spirit directing our prayers and praying (see Romans 8:5).

Effective prayer is only possible if we have renounced all our sins. God hates, no He detests, sin. Until we have a measure of that same feeling for sin, we will not have effective prayers.

People hold on to sin, coddle sin, pamper sin, minimize sin, and turn away from sin by putting it on the shelf where it will wait until the next time. Renounce means to disown. Effective prayer is effective because God and the man or woman of prayer, detest sin.

We have opportunities to pray for changes for the world around us. There are needs of people, churches, ministries, and nations that require men and women of prayer who will seek God for help in time of need. Effective prayer brings real change and what we need today is men and women who can and will pray effective prayers.

Let us pray!

Walking in Effective Prayer, Unit Four, is that prayer which obtains the blessing sought by prayer; answers for our personal need, for the needs of others, and answers on a larger scale, church wide, city wide, and even nation wide. The highest forms of effective prayer are prayers for the needs of others. When we give of our life for the good of others, we have a special place of hearing with God. He delights to listen and then answer our prayers. How will you respond to God's call for prayer? Will you give of your life for effective prayer?

Article 22

A KEY TO SUCCESS

They are everywhere, signs here, signs there, on every tree and pole. Most are hand written and not to fancy, but they proclaim a great opportunity that no one should miss. It is a yard sale!

For some people this is like waving a red towel in front of a bull. They must stop and shop, they know this yard has treasures beyond compare. This is the sale they have been waiting for; they are going to make a great find and get it for a great price. A block away there is another sale waiting, it is the best sale of all time and one where they must stop and shop, another block, another sale, and so on. A great sale is a wonderful event, to find something they want or need is enjoyable; to get it at a great price is electric.

The Bible tells us of making great finds at yard sales. What, you thought yard sales were a new thing? No way. They go way back, Solomon was right, there is nothing new under the sun; there have been yard sales since the beginning of time. In the time of Jesus they were common, men and women searched through the wares offered to find things of value. For example,

139

there is the merchant seeking beautiful pearls. Jesus uses this story to tell His disciples about the great value of the Kingdom of Heaven and how to seek it.

> *Again, the kingdom of heaven is like a merchant seeking beautiful pearls, who, when he had found one pearl of great price, went and sold all that he had and bought it.*
>
> MATTHEW 13:45-46 (NKJV)

When we find something of great value we go to great lengths to obtain it. We might save or work so we have the money to buy it. However, in this case, the pearl was of such great value that the merchant sold all he had (Do you suppose he had a yard sale?). Often, great value will take great effort or cost, but the result is special. In this article I wish to offer you a pearl of great value for effective prayer.

Jesus is the best example of a man of effective prayer. His prayer life was what we long for and aspire to. He received answers and those answers were very powerful and useful for meeting the needs of the situations presented to Him. Please remember that when Jesus was here, He lived as a man. He was fully man and He leaned fully on the Holy Spirit, just as you and I should and must do. With the help of the Holy Spirit we can live and pray as Jesus did, so it is good for us to emulate His life of prayer. It is wise to take note of what He did and work to make His practices our own.

> *who, in the days of His flesh, when He had offered up prayers and supplications, with vehement cries and tears to Him who was able to save Him from death, and was*

heard because of His godly fear, though He was a Son, yet
He learned obedience by the things which He suffered.

HEBREWS 5:7-8 (NKJV)

Answer to prayer is a wonderful thing and a key to getting answers is being heard by God. There are many factors of being heard by God, guarding the condition of the heart, forgiveness, praying in the will of God, and dealing with unbelief, to name a few. Another factor of being heard is seen in the life of Jesus, in this verse from Hebrews. Here we see that Jesus was heard because of His godly fear.

Jesus was heard because of His godly fear; this is a very powerful statement. Under the inspiration of the Holy Spirit the writer of Hebrews says that Jesus was heard because of this fear. Jesus, the sinless Son of God, considered it necessary to fear God. If Jesus was successful because He feared God, how much more do we need to have a healthy fear of the Lord?

People struggle with this concept of fear of the Lord and thereby miss this key for effective prayer. The fear of the Lord is not natural fear, like a rollercoaster ride or a soldier going into battle. The fear of the Lord is not demonic fear, which is from Satan, not God, it holds people back from God and doing what God wants, and it comes with torment, like claustrophobia. The fear of the Lord is not religious fear, which is taught by man. Religious fear is superficial (dealing with outward conduct and not the heart of man), and it has slavish obedience, not free obedience motivated by love of God. The fear of the Lord is not the fear of man, which makes man more important than God, it holds people back from obedience to God, it ensnares people, and it is the opposite of trusting God.

For God has not given us a spirit of fear, but of power and of love and of a sound mind.

2 TIMOTHY 1:7 (NKJV)

Therefore the Lord said: Inasmuch as these people draw near with their mouths And honor Me with their lips, But have removed their hearts far from Me, And their fear toward Me is taught by the commandment of men,

ISAIAH 29:13 (NKJV)

The fear of man brings a snare, But whoever trusts in the Lord shall be safe.

PROVERBS 29:25 (NKJV)

The fear of the Lord is an awe and reverence of God. A good way to understand this is to look at and apply the first commandment, "You shall have no gods before me." Having no god before Our Father requires putting God first in our life, in all things. We are not to have anything before Him; we are not to put any person, thing, or influence before God. This is a reasonable command, as God has given us salvation and all that comes with it. So we should not presume to negate His command or give Him less than the premier place in our life.

You shall have no other gods before Me.

EXODUS 20:3 (NKJV)

"Teacher, which is the great commandment in the law?" Jesus said to him, "'You shall love the Lord your God with all your heart, with all your soul, and with all your mind.' This is the first and great commandment. And the second is like it: 'You shall love your neighbor as yourself.'

On these two commandments hang all the Law and the Prophets."

MATTHEW 22:36-40 (NKJV)

As Christians we are quick to declare that we have no other gods. We proudly proclaim we have no God, but God. However, in practice it is very easy to put other things before God. These things can be objects or people; they can be ideas or desires. When we are challenged by events of life, if we choose these things over the will of God, then they have become a god to us before God.

Two of the most common of these gods that try to take God's rightful place are, our will and our fears. The battle of wills, my will verses God's will, is a common, complex, and thorny struggle. To die to self is commanded by God, but is often more difficult in execution.

We want to have the benefits promised by God, but we long to rule over our life as we see fit. Our old man, our natural nature and flesh, want to be king over what is sometimes called the Kingdom of Self. When we allow our will to rule over God's will, we have placed a god before God. When we do this we are not walking in the fear of the Lord and we hinder the effectiveness of our prayers. Jesus battled over wills and made God's will the winner over His will. With the help of the Holy Spirit we need to do the same.

saying, "Father, if it is Your will, take this cup away from Me; nevertheless not My will, but Yours, be done."

LUKE 22:42 (NKJV)

A second god that tries to take its place before God is fear. Fear can take many forms, but as Derek Prince has said, "What you fear most is your God". We stand in danger of responding to events, pressures, and needs with fear; the fear of the demonic, the fear of religious pressures and persuasion, or the fear of man. These fears can become gods in our life and take the place of God. However, if we cultivate and hold tight to the fear of the Lord, then these other gods will not have His place and we will have success in life and prayer.

> *For the thing I greatly feared has come upon me, And what I dreaded has happened to me.*
>
> JOB 3:25 (NKJV)

> *Then the churches throughout all Judea, Galilee, and Samaria had peace and were edified. And walking in the fear of the Lord and in the comfort of the Holy Spirit, they were multiplied.*
>
> ACTS 9:31 (NKJV)

We can declare our belief of the fear of the Lord. However, in reality this is something that we must nurture in our life and thinking. We cultivate the fear of the Lord because we love God, because of His great gift of salvation, and knowing that our work will be judged. We also develop the fear of the Lord in our life because we long to be effective in prayer. We know that God heard the prayers of Jesus because of His godly fear and He will hear our prayers because of our fear of the Lord.

> *And if you call on the Father, who without partiality judges according to each one's work, conduct yourselves throughout the time of your stay here in fear; knowing that you were not redeemed with corruptible things, like silver or gold, from your aimless conduct received by tradition from your fathers, but with the precious blood*

of Christ, as of a lamb without blemish and without spot.

1 PETER 1:17-19 (NKJV)

Jesus learned obedience and so we, as sons or daughters, must learn obedience. An important part of obedience is obedience to the first commandment, allowing no gods before God. Here is a pearl of great value; daily checking to be certain that no god has been placed before God. This is walking in the fear of the Lord. If we learn this lesson and cultivate good practices of obedience by placing our affections in the correct order with God first, then we will have our prayers heard by God.

Now this is the confidence that we have in Him, that if we ask anything according to His will, He hears us. And if we know that He hears us, whatever we ask, we know that we have the petitions that we have asked of Him.

1 JOHN 5:14-15 (NKJV)

Therefore, since we are receiving a kingdom which cannot be shaken, let us have grace, by which we may serve God acceptably with reverence and godly fear.

HEBREWS 12:28 (NKJV)

Let us pray!

A PATHWAY TO SUCCESS

My Grandparents on my mother's side of the family were remarkable; both Grandpa and Grandma had areas of expertise and together they made a great team. Grandpa was gifted in being able to visualize a tool or process and then make what was needed. My Grandma was a dreamer; she always had ideas for new products.

For example, Grandma invented frozen cookie dough, where a mother could take a package out of the freezer, slice the cookies she wanted, and bake them. Every one has products like this now, but in the early 1950s this was something new. When she wanted to began production, my Grandpa designed the plant for making and packaging these cookies. Together they made a very good team.

In another example of her ideas and his making it happen, My Grandma had an idea for a special gift store called Calico Kate's. The store was so popular that people came to shop from all over America. At one point she had a store near Estes Park, Colorado, plus one in Scottsdale, Arizona, and another in Disneyland in California.

My Grandma was constantly planning new things to do and new products for her store. She had specially made candies and preserves, but the most unusual item was watermelon pickles. This was the rind of watermelons, pickled and preserved in a jar. Most of the food items were purchased from suppliers and given special labels, but the pickles were made at the store.

My Grandpa designed and built a special kitchen just for producing watermelon pickles. If you followed his exact pathway, prepared for a step-by-step process around the room, and knew the secret ingredients, you could produce dozens and dozens of jars of watermelon pickles. When I was a teenager, canning pickles became my summer job. Everything had to be done just the way my Grandpa planned the process; this was the pathway to success.

Just like my Grandpa who designed special equipment and plans for making watermelon pickles, so our Heavenly Father has made a special plan for prayer. If we follow His plan, if we follow His procedures, we will have great success. Learning to be effective in prayer is learning to walk along His pathway to success. It is not surprising God would provide a path to success for every aspect of life, including prayer. He knows people struggle with spiritual things and without detailed and specific guidance and training, people could not be successful. So this pathway is a path to effective prayer.

In the previous article, we describe the fear of the Lord as, placing God first in all we think and do. Anything that would take His place hinders our fellowship with God and our prayers. Many things in the world try to take the place that should be reserved for God. They appeal to our flesh, our mind, our fears, our desires. However, they are all pretenders for the throne of our life and that spot, the prime place, must be reserved for and held for God. God will not go along with any other god ruling and reigning in our life. This is His prerogative and He makes this command for our benefit.

> *My son, if you receive my words, And treasure my commands within you, So that you incline your ear to wisdom, And apply your heart to understanding; Yes, if you cry out for discernment, And lift up your voice for understanding, If you seek her as silver, And search for her as for hidden treasures; Then you will understand the fear of the Lord, And find the knowledge of God.*
>
> *For the Lord gives wisdom; From His mouth come knowledge and understanding; He stores up sound wisdom for the upright; He is a shield to those who walk uprightly; He guards the paths of justice, And preserves the way of His saints. Then you will understand righteousness and justice, Equity and every good path.*
>
> PROVERBS 2:1-9 (NKJV)

The last few lines of these verses are important for people who desire to walk knowing God's will for their life, have a victorious Christian life, and have an effective prayer life. First the Lord gives wisdom. Please note this is not the wisdom of the world, this wisdom is from God and comes only through the spirit. It is God speaking, spirit to spirit, with our spirit.

The wisdom of the world will fail; it is weak, incomplete, and subject to interpretation by our senses through which we receive it. By contrast, the wisdom from God is perfect; it comes with His foreknowledge and blessing. He has a reservoir of sound wisdom stored for all who walk upright before Him. The phrase, sound wisdom, in the Hebrew means to substantiate, support, to have ability. It is help and understanding for us in the things we do.

God gives knowledge and understanding; once again, please do not minimize this. Remember this is the God who created the world we live in, He knows the secrets hidden within. With His help, we can search out and know the secrets.

> *It is the glory of God to conceal a matter, But the glory of kings is to search out a matter.*
>
> PROVERBS 25:2 (NKJV)

Of great importance for success in life and prayer is God's provision for our daily walk. God is the protector of those who walk, what the second chapter of Proverbs calls, upright. The walk of the upright is a walk of prosperity, in all things. The Holy Spirit guides and directs every aspect of our life. We no longer are ruled by our body, emotions, self will, or old ways of thinking. This is prosperity on a level few have even imagined, far above the puny desires of most people.

> *Beloved, I pray that you may prosper in all things and be in health, just as your soul prospers.*
>
> 3 JOHN 1:2 (NKJV)

Finally, God has prepared a path for those who fear Him and walk upright before Him. This is a path he guards for us, and preserves. It is the way of truth, justice, and equity. It is a good path through the mountains of evil that surround us. It is a path we may walk, where the pent-up furry of pressure from fear and worldliness cannot reach us. This is a path where the brilliance of the God's presence guides us and is the luminous beacon of our way.

But the path of the just is like the shining sun, That
shines ever brighter unto the perfect day.

PROVERBS 4:18 (NKJV)

Walking on this path is of high value and like the merchant who found a pearl of great value and sold all he had to buy it, so we must search for and seek out this path. We must work at remaining on this path when we find it. How do we find this path? It comes by the fear of the Lord and walking uprightly before Him. How are we to do this?

Yes, if you cry out for discernment, And lift up your voice
for understanding, If you seek her as silver, And search
for her as for hidden treasures; Then you will understand
the fear of the Lord, And find the knowledge of God.

PROVERBS 2:3-5 (NKJV)

God's instructions are to cry out for discernment or understanding. This is not a whisper or silent prayer, but is calling out with our voice, asking God for these things. We are to actively search for and striving after these things, like we would if great wealth was made available for our taking. This is seeking diligently and fervently, just the way we would if we heard that the Denver mint was giving free samples of gold and silver to everyone who could find the location of the give away.

God's instructions tell us to search like we are looking for hidden treasure. Think of the effort of men looking for sunken treasure from ships lost at sea. Rumor states that there are chest filled with treasure, gold and jewels. However, the location is not certain and as the ship is at the bottom of the sea it takes diligent effort to find and recover the riches. With this same type of effort we must search.

Searching in this case is not so much the location, we know God has what we seek. Searching here is finding the place of walking with God and separate from walking in the world and her ways. The Devil seeks to deter, delay, and defeat your search. He knows that those who find this treasure are dangerous. When you find this path you walk in a realm know only to a few people; you pray with a power no man, mountain, or nation can stand against. Seek the path God has prepared for you. Seek with all of your heart.

Let us pray!

WISDOM

I love to read! For years I have said that my dream job would be to get paid for reading. I would want it to be a well paid position and I would not have any restriction on what I picked to read. This would be wonderful. There are so many books I would like to read, I always have several books on my "to read" shelf.

I enjoy a lot of books, but the best book I read is the Bible. It also has a pedigree that no other book can match; it is the Word of God. It is the perfect guide to life and living, and it reads me as I read it. By that I mean that it is like a mirror showing me what I look like in action and beliefs. It presents the perfect standard and then shows the careful reader, where he or she comes short and what to do to come up to the high standard. It is a great book!

The Bible is filled with wonderful stories like those in the book of Daniel. I love the story of the fourth man in the fire with Hananiah, Mishael, and Azariah (Shadrack, Meshach, and Abed-Nego). To come out of the fire without even the smell of smoke, is a mighty work of the God we serve. And He is still doing mighty works for those who seek Him and His ways!

Who has not been challenged to the very core of his life, beliefs, and actions, by the story of the handwriting on the wall? The life of the king was placed before the mirror of the Word and judgment came. The interpretation of these words was given by Daniel.

> *"And this is the inscription that was written: MENE, MENE, TEKEL, UPHARSIN. This is the interpretation of each word. Mene: God has numbered your kingdom, and finished it; Tekel: You have been weighed in the balances, and found wanting; Peres: Your kingdom has been divided, and given to the Medes and Persians."*
>
> DANIEL 5:25-28 (NKJV)

This leads us to the question, what about hand writing on our wall? What will God find in us and what will He write about us? You have been weighed in the balance and found... Please remember this is going to happen to each of us, our works will be judged by God. What will He say of you, "Well?" or "Well done!"

These are very powerful stories. The story that fits with the focus of this article is also found in Daniel, this time in the second chapter of the book. This is the story of king Nebuchadnezzar and his dreams. He wanted to know the meaning of these dreams and no one could tell him. So he decreed the death of all magicians, astrologers, and sorcerers. However, God had other plans; He told Daniel in a vision the dream and its interpretation. Read, once again, the words of Daniel as he blessed God for revealing the dream and interpretation.

> *Then the secret was revealed to Daniel in a night vision. So Daniel blessed the God of heaven. Daniel answered and said: "Blessed be the name of God forever and ever, For wisdom and might are His. And He changes the times and the seasons; He removes kings and raises up kings; He gives wisdom to the wise And knowledge to those who have understanding. He reveals deep and secret things; He knows what is in the darkness, And light dwells with Him. "I thank You and praise You, O God of my fathers; You have given me wisdom and might, And have now made known to me what we asked of You, For You have made known to us the king's demand."*
>
> DANIEL 2:19-23 (NKJV)

Daniel praised God for giving wisdom. Throughout the Bible the value and importance of wisdom is proclaimed. Please note, and this is very important, the wisdom given to Daniel was not the wisdom of man. The wisest men of Nebuchadnezzar's kingdom did not have the wisdom needed for the king. No amount of training and learning would be enough for this occasion; only the wisdom of God was sufficient.

Prayer ranges from a simple cry unto the Lord, to prayers that are mighty to the pulling down of strongholds. Prayer can be powerful beyond the strength of anything designed by man. Many people are satisfied with simple prayers; they are comforted and reassured. Others want more from prayer. They see the record and know that God has moved mightily in response to prayer. They see God deliver and save from calamity. They see nations turned and mighty armies defeated. They see light brought to dark places and revival come to a hardened place.

What makes the difference? There are several things, the desire of those who want to pray, the heart attitude they cultivate with the help of the Holy Spirit, and the destruction of unbelief, so faith can be strong and rule over their thoughts, statements, and actions. They have a humbleness that seeks the will of the Father over their will, and willingness to forgive even as they are forgiven. They will not be moved by circumstances, rules, appearances, traditions, or threats. They believe God is willing and able to do what He promises.

> *The earnest (heartfelt, continued) prayer of a righteous man makes tremendous power available—dynamic in its working"*
>
> JAMES 5:17 (AMPLIFIED BIBLE)

Another key to powerful prayer, one that is often missing or miss applied, is wisdom. Too often we acquiesce to the wisdom of man, when what we need is the wisdom of God. The wisdom of man cannot compare to the wisdom of God. The wisdom of man results in weak, anemic prayers that avail little. The wisdom of God results in prayers of power and effectiveness. Today we need powerful effective prayers and to have this we must have the wisdom of God directing and empowering our prayers.

Where does the wisdom of God come from? How did Daniel acquire it and how can we? The answer is easy Job explains it to us.

> *"From where then does wisdom come? And where is the place of understanding? It is hidden from the eyes of all living, And concealed from the birds of the air.*

Destruction and Death say, 'We have heard a report about it with our ears.' God understands its way, And He knows its place. For He looks to the ends of the earth, And sees under the whole heavens, To establish a weight for the wind, And apportion the waters by measure. When He made a law for the rain, And a path for the thunderbolt, Then He saw wisdom and declared it; He prepared it, indeed, He searched it out. And to man He said, 'Behold, the fear of the Lord, that is wisdom, And to depart from evil is understanding.'"

JOB 28:20-28 (NKJV)

From where does wisdom come? It comes from the fear of the Lord and to depart from evil. There are several key points we must understand if we are going to have and apply the wisdom of God in our prayers. First there is no other source. In the previous articles of this book, we have seen that the fear of the Lord is placing God first in our life, thoughts, actions, and beliefs. When anything else is placed before Him or even beside Him, we do not have the proper requirements for the fear of the Lord and it will not be active in our life. The man or woman that has other gods before God, does not have the fear of the Lord, and will not have the wisdom of God.

Our second main point here is that the wisdom of God and a departure from evil are linked. We see this in this passage from Job and in many others. The fear of the Lord is placing God first in our life, and this requires a departure from evil.

The Bible states that if I regard iniquity in my heart, I will receive nothing from God. This iniquity is actually a god that I have placed before God; thus I do not have the fear of the Lord. To have the wisdom of God in our life and prayers, we must, by the help of the Word of God and guidance of the Holy Spirit, depart from evil.

> *And to man He said, 'Behold, the fear of the Lord, that is wisdom, And to depart from evil is understanding.'"*
>
> JOB 28:28 (NKJV)

The third point is that the wisdom of God is not the same as the wisdom of man. You might say that is obvious, God knows more. However, it is more than just God knows more. His wisdom is of an entirely different class from the wisdom of man.

The wisdom of man comes through and functions in the soulish part of man, which contains the will, emotions, and mind. The wisdom of man comes through the senses to the mind. There is value in education, but education does not bring us the wisdom of God. Please note, Job writes that wisdom is "hidden from the eyes of all living". And David writes that wisdom comes to the inward and hidden parts of man. This is from the Spirit of God to the spirit of man.

> *Behold, You desire truth in the inward parts, And in the hidden part You will make me to know wisdom.*
>
> PSALM 51:6 (NKJV)

Derek Prince explains, "The wisdom of God is unique, it is something entirely on its own it comes into the spirit and enables us to see God's purposes, to see our life and the things around us in the light of God's purpose and God's council. Council is something very closely tied to wisdom in scripture. When we have this kind of wisdom, we receive God's council, we know how to act in different situations, we know how to relate to different people, and we know how to help people"

From a *Legacy Radio* broadcast *The Fear of the Lord*, by Derek Prince

The wisdom of God made all the difference for Daniel. He answered the king; he was kept from death, and promoted to high position. The wisdom of God changes our prayers from limitation of man to the unlimited knowledge and understanding of God. God knows the times and seasons of man, churches, and nations. With His wisdom we can pray powerful effective prayers.

Let us pray!

EXPECTATION

Living life with me can be difficult at times. One example of this is when I am preparing for a mission trip. I get so excited about the trip that I talk about the trip all the time. I am almost as bad as the man who talked and talked about himself and then said, "Well enough about me, let's talk about some thing else. What do you think about me?" When my wife and I go to dinner, we talk about the trip, when we ride in the car, we talk about the trip. Then for a change of pace, I ask my wife what she thinks about the trip. You see, I told you I can be difficult.

Why do I get so excited about going on a trip? I like trips and travel, I like seeing places far from home. I like seeing friends. I like to help others and serve them for Christ. But please note, and this is the theme of this article, I get excited because I expect to go on the trip. I expect to have a great trip, and I expect to see God do great things. I am excited because I have high expectations.

Prayer is the most powerful force on earth. By prayer we can set the course of our life or the course of the life for a family, church, or nation. God's promises concerning prayer are so powerful that most people simply cannot take it in. They reject the promises or strive to limit the meaning and power. However, for those who long to see the mighty power of God at work in their life, effective prayer is a worthwhile goal to pursue.

Because it is so powerful and important, one of the most desperate needs for people and nations, today, is men and women of effective prayer. The opportunities that stretch out before us are too vast and too important for anything other than effective prayer. Nothing, but the believing man or woman of effective prayer, will reach God and His power in the ways and means necessary for meeting needs.

People interested in prayer, look at many factors for success. Faith, seeking God, the Word of God, the attitude of our heart, forgiveness, limiting fear and doubt, and other factors are all important and worthy of our study. It is a true statement that the man or woman of effective prayer will be working to have all of these factors properly dealt with or properly in force in their life and their prayer life. Without seeking God and all of these factors that come from a close relationship with the Father, our prayer life will be impotent. This is one of the reasons that a prayer life is so important; it is impossible to be successful in prayer without the working of the Holy Spirit changing us from the inside out. The man or woman of prayer must be a new creation in Christ in fact and practice, not just in name.

There is another factor, one that is often overlooked, but it is a key to our success, it is high expectation. I expected to go and be blessed spiritually and physically on trips and to be a blessing. My faith works because I expect to see great things happen, for me and through me. If we are going to have success in prayer we must have high expectation of God doing what He has promised in answer to prayers. Look at this statement of Solomon. Please note carefully and prayerfully what he is saying.

> *And he said: "Blessed be the Lord God of Israel, who has fulfilled with His hands what He spoke with His mouth to my father David,*
>
> 2 CHRONICLES 6:4 (NKJV)

This should and must be our expectation of what God will do with our prayers. Solomon said; God has done what David asked. We need to have expectation that God will do what we have asked. Until we have this expectation we limit our faith and prayers. Without expectation we are not looking for answers, we are not planning for answers, and we are not going to receive answers to our prayers. Look at your prayer life; you do have a prayer life, right, what are your expectations?

Most people, who pray, claim to have expectations of answers from God. They express their belief that God answers prayers. However, from this initial and often vague claim, there often is a breakdown in expectations. What people claim as expectations, is really just "hoping and wishing". They talk and talk, and then talk some more, but they do not have expectation of answers from God. They hope He will do something, they wish for answers, but they do not have expectation of receiving answers and so no faith is applied to their prayers and they do not get an answer. How do we know this, their actions and words reveal their lack of expectation.

When I am going on a trip, I have expectation of going. I begin to do things. I check my passport, I buy airline tickets, I call my friends, I set up an itinerary, I buy the currency of the country where I am going, I check health and safety regulations, I get out my suitcase, as a mater of fact I have a list of things I do. Why do I do these things, because of expectation, I expect to go on the trip.

Too often, in prayer, we pray, but we do not have expectation of getting answers. Oh, sure we might hope that God will do something, but our expectation is so low we do not act. For most people when it comes to prayer, if they have expectation at all, they act on their expectation that nothing will happen from their prayers. Some do not believe that God answers prayers. Some believe He only answers the prayers of special people, and some don't know what to believe. So what do they do? They continue their life just as they have been, not expecting God to answer. They do not expect their prayers to avail anything, let alone much.

It is not just actions that speak loudly of their lack of expectations, their words say, "NO EXPECTATION". Their words are doubt, fear, denial, sin, unbelief, ridicule, and/or unforgiveness. The things they say are a declaration that they have no expectation of God answering their prayers. Even if there is a particle of expectation at the prayer meeting, they negate this before they reach their car, by what they say. Things like, "I am glad we prayed about God healing and blessing with health, at this meeting, because I always get the flu. I will probably be sick by the end of the week." There is no expectation of answers to their prayers or even of the prayers of others.

To have expectation of answers we must deal with the things that hinder or destroy expectation. On the positive side there are things we should and must do if we are going to have high expectation and allow faith to work in our prayer life. By the work and guidance of the Holy Spirit we can change our expectation, or lack there of, to high expectation of God work-ing mightily in our life and prayers.

We need to study, meditate, and walk in the love of the Father. The love of God is His drawing card, it leads us to re-pentance, it leads us to salvation, and it leads us to works of service. It is the love of God that grows in us, so that there are changes to our thinking and actions. The love of God moti-vates and invigorates the recognition of and desire for the great promises and deeds of God.

Power in prayer begins with the love of God and it takes prayer to its highest place that of praying for the good of others. When we walk in the love of God, His promises are fulfilled, we see His love motivating, and we see His power working. By His love we seek God's will in all we do and in our prayers. When we fully enter into His will, we can ask for anything and He will do it. This brings high expectation for answers to prayers.

We need to study, meditate, and walk in the promises of God. It is so important that we know what God has promised and know what His record is concerning what He has done. There are few things that are better for building high expecta-tion, than hearing what God has done. God the Father has a record of answering prayers that is awesome. Feed on this re-cord, read of His promises, next read the prayers of people and note the answers from God. This brings high expectation for answers to prayers.

We need to study, meditate, and walk in who Christ is and who we are in Him. The man, who does not know that he is an heir, thinks and acts differently from the man who knows. We can have high expectation, if we know what Christ has done. His work is mighty to defeating our enemy and every foe. Our position in Christ, as joint heirs with Him, is one of position and power. We have access with the Father and this access is for bold entry and asking in faith, for answer to all our petitions. If we know who we are and to whom we belong, we can ask with faith. This brings high expectation for answers to prayers.

We need to study, meditate, and walk in aids to stopping bad actions, that is, actions that hinder or stop high expectation of answers to our prayers. God has called us to walk a holy life and this is especially true for those who will pray effective prayers. He has given us all we need to be willing and able to walk holy. His demand of a holy walk, is not just an idle statement, but reflects His requirements and what He knows we need to have, to have power in prayer. Walking in His holiness will change our life and prayers. This brings high expectation for answers to prayers.

We need to study, meditate, and walk in ways that put a guard to our mouth so we say what we should and only what we should. There is no area where more people destroy their faith and expectation than this. They do not watch what they say. Our tongue can be our best friend or worst enemy; it all depends on how it is used.

Unfortunately for most people the tongue is an enemy. We sound like the world, saying the things the world says, and so we get the results of the world, death and destruction. What we should be saying, to walk with God and be effective in prayer, is affirming His power, might, ability, love, and concern, and our position of favor with Him. This brings high expectation for answers to prayers.

Prayer is hard for many people because of their level of expectation. Why spend the time and effort if you expect nothing in return. So with this low expectation of success few people pray and fewer still pray effective prayers. However, this is not

God's plan or will. He is looking for people who by reason of their training have high expectation of answers to their prayers. Jesus' expectation was that God always heard His prayer. He knew that if God heard he would answer. This same high expectation is the expectation He has for us that we would pray, be heard and have answers to our prayers. This is high expectation of answers to our prayers.

Let us pray!

FAITH IN

W hile I was stationed in Germany in the US Air Force, I was invited to go with a group, lead by a several chaplains from military bases in Europe, to Israel. It was a great trip; we saw many of the key sites of Jerusalem and Israel, and went to a wonderful conference in Jerusalem and Tel Aviv. The visit to places mentioned in the Bible was very special. It was wonderful to see where people of the Bible had lived and worked. It was fantastic to walk where Jesus walked. It brought the stories to life.

One of the places we traveled, was the town of Sychar the site of Jacob's well. Here the story of the Samaritan Woman who met Jesus at the well flooded over us. You could almost hear Jesus telling this woman all about her life.

In this story, the woman and then later the people of the town had a powerful encounter with Jesus. After Jesus and the woman had talked, John's account tells us that she went and told the people, "Come, see a Man who told me all the things that I ever did". The people of Sychar came out and talked with Jesus. After they had talked with Him, they said, "Now we believe, not because of what you said, for we ourselves have heard Him".

The most important key to successful prayer is relationship with God. Without access to Him and His willingness to listen to our prayers, there is no prayer. The second most important key is faith. The lessons of faith well learned and applied, change prayer, from a religious duty to the joy of walking and working in concert with our Father, and in great power.

Most teachings on faith deal with the speaking and doing aspects of faith. And what we say and do makes a huge difference in having and using faith. We can destroy our faith if we do not say the right things. People, too often, agree with circumstances and the world, over what God and the Bible say. So they get nothing by faith. The same is true with our actions. People often act under the pressure of the circumstances and the world, and defeat faith. They do not act on faith; they act on fear, doubt, and unbelief.

If we are going to have success in prayer, we must say and do what the Bible directs. However, there is more to faith than just speaking and doing. Understanding this more fully will help us to walk in faith and have powerful prayers.

There is a difficulty that most people must address; they are not sure what faith is. They know the catch phrases, they can say the right words, but their understanding is clouded at best. We know that, "Now faith is the substance of things hoped for, the evidence of things not seen" (Hebrews 11:1 (NKJV)). And for most people this leaves them with a vague longing for faith, but not a clear understanding of what faith is and more importantly, what is needed for faith to operate in their life and prayers.

One of the most powerful passages on prayer in the Bible is found in Mark chapter 11. Jesus' teaching speaks of unlimited power in prayer. This is a very powerful promise.

> *Therefore I say to you, whatever things you ask when you pray, believe that you receive them, and you will have them.*
>
> MARK 11:24 (NKJV)

It is important to understand that the strength of a promise is based on the person making the promise. We have more faith in a promise that is made by a person we know and trust. A promise is powerful when it comes from one who is capable and willing to do what he promises.

The story of the events at Jacob's well, can help us more fully understand this. In the story, the woman told the people, come and see, later the people said, we have heard. Here are two important ingredients in faith, see and hear. For effective faith we must see and hear God.

Notice that before Jesus gives the promise of power in prayer in Mark chapter 11, He tells His disciples to "Have faith in God." The beginning of faith is faith in God. He is the surety and power making good the promise. We can and must believe that God is and that He will do what He has promised. Effective faith is faith in God and in His promises.

Just as the woman at the well was so impressed with Jesus that she went and told the people to come and see. So we must be impressed with God, by seeing Him. It is in His presence that we see His nature and faithfulness. When we see Him, we can have faith. The Bible gives us a great example of this principle, Paul's faith was not in a creed, traditions of man, or even in rumors. Paul was the great man of faith because he knew Jesus.

> *For this reason I also suffer these things; nevertheless I am not ashamed, for I know whom I have believed and am persuaded that He is able to keep what I have committed to Him until that Day.*
>
> 2 TIMOTHY 1:12 (NKJV)

Believing God is simply looking at God and what He is, and allowing Him to reveal His presence to us. Give Him time and completely yield to Him, receiving and rejoicing in His love. Faith is the eye through which the light of God's presence and the vigor of His power stream into the soul. As that which I see lives in me, so by faith God lives in me, too.

From *With Christ in the School of Prayer* by Andrew Murray
We also need to hear His voice and allow it to fill our heart. One of the limitations, of the use of email, is not hearing the voice of the person we are dealing with. We depend greatly on hearing the voice of the other person to know what they are really saying. This is also true with hearing God. His voice is the voice of authority, love, blessing, correction, provision, answers, guidance, and comfort; it is all this and more because His voice reflects who and what He is. We can have great faith, if we hear His voice. He is speaking great promises to us and by his voice we know that He is faithful, He will do what He says.

> *It is the Spirit who gives life; the flesh profits nothing. The words that I speak to you are spirit, and they are life.*
>
> JOHN 6:63 (NKJV)

But as it is written: "Eye has not seen, nor ear heard, Nor have entered into the heart of man The things which God has prepared for those who love Him." But God has revealed them to us through His Spirit. For the Spirit searches all things, yes, the deep things of God.

I CORINTHIANS 2:9-10 (NKJV)

Faith in the promise is the fruit of faith in the promiser. The prayer of faith is rooted in the life of faith. And in this way the faith that prays effectively is indeed a gift from God. It is not something He bestows or infuses all at once, but is far deeper and truer. It is the blessed disposition or habit of soul that grows up in us through a life of communion with Him. Surely for one who knows our Father well and lives in constant close communion with Him, it is a simple thing to believe the promise that He will do what His child wishes.

From *With Christ in the School of Prayer* by Andrew Murray

Yet indeed I also count all things loss for the excellence of the knowledge of Christ Jesus my Lord, for whom I have suffered the loss of all things, and count them as rubbish, that I may gain Christ and be found in Him, not having my own righteousness, which is from the law, but that which is through faith in Christ, the righteousness which is from God by faith; that I may know Him and the power of His resurrection, and the fellowship of His sufferings, being conformed to His death, if, by any means, I may attain to the resurrection from the dead.

PHILIPPIANS 3:8-11 (NKJV)

God is faithful, by whom you were called into the fellowship of His Son, Jesus Christ our Lord.

1 CORINTHIANS 1:9 (NKJV)

So Jesus answered and said to them, "Have faith in God".

MARK 11:22 (NKJV)

Our faith is based on God's promises and His willingness and ability to fulfill His promises for us. Without the seeing of our eyes and hearing of our ears, our heart will not be filled with the promises of God, have faith in God, or be filled with faith. With the seeing of our eyes and hearing of our ears, we can have confidence in God and be full of faith. When we are full of faith, we can have effective prayers.

Let us pray!

THE OLD BARN

The snow drifts, fueled by 50 to 70 mile an hour winds, were 20 feet deep in places. Sub zero temperatures continued for several days. People froze to death in their homes. Hundreds of people were stranded and had to wait for the storm to pass, staying with people who kindly opened their homes. This was the Blizzard of '49. Actually the winter of 1948 and 49 had several blizzards. November 18 and 19 of 1948 most of northern Colorado suffered under the grip of a massive blizzard. By Thanksgiving most of the snow had melted and December was warmer than usual. Then early on January 2, 1949 and continuing for three days was the worst blizzard to hit Colorado since 1888.

In 1945 my Grandpa went to work for Consumers Oil Company driving a propane truck. He delivered propane to a wide area of northern Colorado. He had struggled through the blizzard in November of '48 working to get propane to tanks his records indicated would be low. However, his stories of what happened this January are even more incredible.

Once again he knew that several farms would soon be low on propane, so he joined with the county road crews working to cut lanes through the snow drifts and they began going to farm houses. They would cut their way through, taking supplies and propane to grateful farm families.

At one farm, the family was grateful for the help, and the farmer asked for help to get to his barn. He had tried to maintain a clear path, but could not keep up with the wind blown snow. Between his house and the barn there were drifts 12 feet high.

They cut a path with the heavy road grading equipment and as they got close they could hear the cows bellowing. When they opened the doors all they saw was a wall of snow. They went around to the back of the barn, to the opening of the second level loft, and finally they could see into the barn. And before them were all the cows. As the snow had blown into the barn the cows had packed it down and now they were all the way up to the second level of the barn. The cows were okay, they were very hungry and thirsty, but the barn had protected them through the blizzard.

A good barn is important to a farm. It affords protection for cattle, a workplace, and a storage place for tools and feed. Another important value of the barn is the protection from the wind and cold. Filling a barn with heat takes a lot of work. You can fire up a heater, but this can be very expensive, and on the plains of Colorado most barns do not have heaters. Most of the heat is from the cows and it takes the effort of a lot of cows. Little by little the cows will fill a barn with enough heat to protect them from the cold of a night or a storm. In some ways prayer is like a barn.

Prayer is God's provision for dealing with the conditions and elements around us. We live in a challenging world and face many difficulties. There is much to hinder our faith and work, to steal our strength and provision, and destroy our life. However, like a barn, prayer is a tool for bringing God's life and provision to us and to our neighbors. At times answers to prayers come quickly and with thankfulness we receive from God. Other prayers take longer to receive the answer.

Few people take up God's call to pray. Sure in a moment of disaster people may cry out, but the number of people who truly pray, expecting to be heard by God and have Him answer their prayers, is surprisingly small. This is sad, as there is great power available in prayer, if they would seek God and learn to pray. Of the people who do pray, many struggle with slow or seemingly delayed answers to prayer. It takes great patience and endurance to continue in faith. Difficult as it may be, this is what is needed today; men and women of prayer, who will not quit until they receive the answer from God.

> It is the secret of power and life, not only for ourselves, but for others, for the Church, and for the world. It is to prayer that God has given the right to take hold of Him and His strength. It is on prayer that the promises wait for their fulfillment, the kingdom waits for its coming, and the glory of God waits for its full revelation. How slothful and unfit we are for this blessed work.

From *With Christ in the School of Prayer* by Andrew Murray
Taking hold of God and His strength is the most desperately needed commodity in the world today. We do this by prayer. Prayer is by faith and as we pray in faith, we fill a spiritual prayer bowl. The prayer bowl is mentioned in the book of Revelations. Prayers are prayed, for a specific area of need or concern and slowly the bowl is filled and when filled the

answer comes. In this article, the prayer bowl is like filling the barn, one prayer at a time.

> *Now when He had taken the scroll, the four living creatures and the twenty-four elders fell down before the Lamb, each having a harp, and golden bowls full of incense, which are the prayers of the saints.*
>
> REVELATIONS 5:8 (NKJV)

Barns come in many sizes. Some are so big you could play football or soccer inside. Others are little more than the size of a shed. Obviously it is easier to fill a small shed size barn than a massive mall size barn. Some prayer assignments are shed size, others present more colossal demands. Regardless of the size, filling a prayer barn requires faith. We must know that our Father hears our prayers and listens, and we must also believe that He answers prayer.

Rees Howells asked an important question, when he and millions of other people from Great Britain were called to pray concerning the Battle of Britain. His question, "What if millions prayed, but no one believed?" Prayer without faith is better than not, at least if you pray you will be busy and cannot get in trouble. However, without faith, prayer is just talk. The first key to success in prayer is praying in faith. There is no substitute for faith, regardless of the size of the need; the answer comes only by faith.

The second key to success in prayer is continuing in faith until the answer is manifest. For example, in praying for other people, we must pray in faith and often we must continue in our prayer and stance of faith, sometimes for a long time. The bigger the barn the tougher it is to continue in faith. The world, our flesh, sin, and hindrances, are all tailored made to try and stop our faith.

When you want to heat a barn the first step is to get the cattle inside. The second is to close the door. Keeping the door closed is important; the warming effect is ruined when the door opens. Every time you open the door heat escapes and cold comes in. If you close the door quickly you might not have to start the process over, but you will have to overcome the loss of heat. When we pray and then continue in faith, we must keep the door closed on sin, must keep our mouth closed to bad confession, we must close the door to all actions that obstruct faith.

Perseverance can be the toughest thing we have to do in prayer. It is hard to not say or do faith wrecking things. We must put on the helmet of salvation and using the word of God, pray, and then continue in faith. Then we can see the barn, large or small, filled by prayer. We can see the prayer bowl full and ready for God to pour out His power, strength, and answers.

> *But if we hope for what we do not see, we eagerly wait for it with perseverance.*
>
> ROMANS 8:25 (NKJV)

> *And take the helmet of salvation, and the sword of the Spirit, which is the word of God; praying always with all prayer and supplication in the Spirit, being watchful to this end with all perseverance and supplication for all the saints*
>
> EPHESIANS 6:17-18 (NKJV)

> *to knowledge self-control, to self-control perseverance, to perseverance godliness, to godliness brotherly kindness,*

and to brotherly kindness love. For if these things are yours and abound, you will be neither barren nor unfruitful in the knowledge of our Lord Jesus Christ.

2 PETER 1:6-8 (NKJV)

Let us pray!

THE ARMOR OF VICTORY

Castles can be fascinating and a great way to view history. The Edinburgh castle overlooking Edinburgh, Scotland is one of those wonderful castles like those found many places in Europe. Here, as is found on many castles, at the main gate is a guard of statues of knights in armor. They look great in the armor of the period when they defended the castle. However, for years now they have just stood in place posing for pictures with the tourists.

At one time in history knights were a mighty force for armies. They would ride out to do battle with the enemies of the kingdom. Their armor was designed to give them protection so they could be fearless in battle. Over the years this protection got stronger and better until the knights were fully encased in metal armor and had to be lifted to their armor clad horses. However, through out the evolution of their armor, knights never just stood still. They always did battle.

The victorious Christian life is often portrayed as preparing for and doing battle. Unfortunately too many Christians act like the knights on the castles today, standing in armor, but never leaving their perch or pedestal. Not knowing their position or power in Christ, they are afraid to bother the enemy. They think the best way to survive, is to be as quiet and hidden as possible. They think they can make it through life if they do not bother the enemy. If they do nothing to rile him up, then they will not be attacked. And to make matters worse, the enemy has so buffaloed many Christians they blame God for their problems and not the enemy who attacks, even though they have worked to not disturb him. They do no battle and reap a mediocre life at best and never experience the joy of victory.

The most famous comparison of the Christian life with armor is found in Ephesians chapter six. Paul carefully laid out the various pieces of the Christian's armor; belt, breastplate, boots, shield, helmet, and sword. This armor is the great protection for the Christian; truth, righteousness, gospel of peace, faith, salvation, and the Word of God. This is the great battle armor of the Christian and what Paul expects all Christians to wear.

> *Finally, my brethren, be strong in the Lord and in the*
> *power of His might. Put on the whole armor of God, that*
> *you may be able to stand against the wiles of the devil.*
> *For we do not wrestle against flesh and blood, but against*
> *principalities, against powers, against the rulers of the*
> *darkness of this age, against spiritual hosts of wickedness*
> *in the heavenly places. Therefore take up the whole*
> *armor of God, that you may be able to withstand in the*
> *evil day, and having done all, to stand. Stand therefore,*
> *having girded your waist with truth, having put on the*
> *breastplate of righteousness, and having shod your feet*
> *with the preparation of the gospel of peace; above all,*

taking the shield of faith with which you will be able to
quench all the fiery darts of the wicked one. And take the
helmet of salvation, and the sword of the Spirit, which
is the word of God; praying always with all prayer and
supplication in the Spirit, being watchful to this end with
all perseverance and supplication for all the saints

EPHESIANS 6:10-18 (NKJV)

This is the armor of the great Christian soldier who is marching out to war. Where the problem begins is in people's thinking about the word "stand" found in this passage. Too often it is thought of as a command to not move, or even to remain, like the knights in the castles today, out of the way of the battle. This kind of standing has become an art form, with every aspect of life and living designed to not stir up trouble or offend. People tolerate almost anything, rather than fight against the Devil. And most people are buffeted by him and this seems to be the way it is, a hopeless life.

This hopelessness should not be the Christian's lot in life. The armor is not for standing and taking a beating, it is for doing battle and winning great victories! Too long the Body of Christ has been a doormat to the Devil, allowing him to reap havoc in our life, family, and ministry. This should not be so.

We are the victors, if you do not remember this, read the end of the Bible. It talks about a great victory and we are a part of winning the war. We have great armor and weapons that are mighty and designed for victory. We must change and stop thinking we are weak and helpless. We must rise up and do battle and win! Our victories are to overcome the attacks of the Devil here and now! The weapons of our warfare are mighty. God has given us all we need to win. We have the armor for protection and the Word of God for attack.

The power for a Christian warrior is the Word of God. And the Word of God is designed for our use in attack. Verses 17 and 18 of the armor passage explain the battle plan. We are to take the helmet of salvation, and the sword of the Spirit, which is the word of God; praying always with all prayer and supplication in the Spirit. The weapons of our warfare are simple, but powerful; speaking and praying the Word of God.

The word translated stand in this passage is not passive, but active. It is the Greek word, "histemi" and means an active stance, to continue to present. One of the definitions of the word "present" is to introduce before a court as an object of inquiry. The idea here expressed is one of continually speaking the Word of God through prayer. Now remember this is a spiritual battle (see verse twelve), and so our job is to put on our armor and speak and pray the Word. Paul in this passage states that we attack by praying the Word of God.

Jesus when tempted by the Devil presented the Word of God. His active attack in the battle was, "It is written, Man shall not live by bread alone, but by every Word of God." Jesus had a great victory over the Devil. The Devil comes around at what he views as an opportune time. When he comes, we must be in battle armor and then turn the battle on him and attack, just as Jesus did. We do this by speaking and praying the Word of God.

If we are at the hospital and the doctor's report is cancer, this is an opportune time for the Devil. He will shout death, hopelessness, certain defeat. He will attack and wipeout the less than vigilant man or woman. Too often the armor is at home in the closet and before we can even think of doing battle we have been wounded. We cry out in pain, despair, and defeat.

When knights wore armor they would suit up on the days they were going out and do battle. Their armor was too heavy and unwieldy to wear it everyday and every where. So they only suited up, mounted their trusted steed and did battle on certain days.

We must prepare for battle. However, we should daily have on our armor. We should plan to do battle and have the victory every day. Before the enemy can attack, we are prepared and when he comes to do battle we are ready. We are armed with great armor and ready with our powerful weapons using the Word of God.

We do not fight fair. We come prepared, we are protected, and we have the ultimate weapon, against which the Devil cannot stand. We follow the three steps to victory. We pray the Word of God. We then continue in prayer by praise and thanksgiving and praying in the Holy Spirit. Then we remain constant in faith by speaking the Word of God with a good confession. The Devil's only option is to get beaten up, a little or a lot!

> *For though we walk in the flesh, we do not war according to the flesh. For the weapons of our warfare are not carnal but mighty in God for pulling down strongholds, casting down arguments and every high thing that exalts itself against the knowledge of God, bringing every thought into captivity to the obedience of Christ, and being ready to punish all disobedience when your obedience is fulfilled.*
>
> 2 CORINTHIANS 10:3-6 (NKJV)

It is time for Christian soldiers to rise up and take an active stance. We are to do battle with the Devil and defeat him on every front. For too long the Body of Christ has played the role of weaklings, waiting for a beating. This is a false image of a Christian; it is not what we should be. Now we need to stand up as the victorious Bride of Christ, endued with His power and name. Now is the time for men and women of prayer to have effective, fervent prayers that avail much, not succumbing to the wiles of the Devil, but overcoming by speaking and praying the Word. Jesus brought us into the Kingdom not to get whipped, but to be mighty in battle. We are destined to win and the time for winning is now!

Let us pray!

Prayer for Salvation

Earthquakes and Tsunami, wars and riots, the world is filled with difficult situation. It is easy to be ruled by fear and terror. Every day is a battle to keep from falling victim of dread and anxiety. The Bible reveals that there would be times like these and there is only one answer, Jesus Christ. Dealing with the pressures of today makes this a great time to get to know Him.

These verses from Romans will help us understand how to make a positive change in our life. If you believe in your heart as these verse say, you can be saved. Read the verse and then pray the prayer. Pray with sincerity and trusting God and be born again.

> *that if you confess with your mouth the Lord Jesus and believe in your heart that God has raised Him from the dead, you will be saved. For with the heart one believes unto righteousness, and with the mouth confession is made unto salvation.*
>
> ROMANS 10:9-10 (NKJV)

Dear God in Heaven, I recognize that I am a sinner, and I need help. I come to you in the name of Jesus to receive salvation and eternal life. I believe that Jesus is your Son. I believe that He died on the cross for my sins and that you raised Him from the dead. I receive Jesus now and make Him the Lord of my life. Jesus come to me, I welcome you as my Lord and Savior. Father, I believe Your Word says, that I am now saved. I confess with my mouth that I am saved and born again. I am now a child of God.

Congratulations you are now part of the body of Christ!

Now what should you do?

Tell someone of your decision (you could email me at dave@voiceofthanksgiving.com)

Get a Bible and read it

Find a Christian church that believes the Bible, be an active and faithful participant at meetings

Get baptized

Learn to pray, effective prayers that avail much

Voice of Thanksgiving

The *Voice of Thanksgiving* is a newsletter calling men and women to effective prayer. *Voice of Thanksgiving* is published in a weekly version in English and monthly versions, in German and Polish. Articles from the newsletter and much more can be seen at the *Voice of Thanksgiving* website. This website contains an archive of past issues, a prayer blog, and useful information and resources on prayer, intercession, and victorious Christian living.

The *Voice of Thanksgiving* website can be seen at: http://voiceofthanksgiving.com

To receive *Voice of Thanksgiving* weekly by email, send an e-mail with word JOIN in the subject line to: david@voiceofthanksgiving.com

Prayer: A Force that Causes Change
> *Volume 1 – A Call to Prayer*
> *Volume 2 – A Life of Prayer*
> *Volume 3 – Faithful in Prayer*
> *Volume 4 – Effective Prayer*

Copies of these books are available at:
http://voiceofthanksgiving.com/Book/Book.htm